THE POWER OF
MENTAL
GOLF

IMPROVE YOUR
CONFIDENCE AND CONSISTENCY

T0161456

KERRY R. GRAHAM
LPGA TEACHING & CLUB PROFESSIONAL | HALL OF FAME MEMBER

AND RICKI LINKSMAN, M.ED.
ACCELERATED BRAIN-BASED LEARNING EXPERT

THE POWER OF
MENTAL
GOLF

IMPROVE YOUR
CONFIDENCE AND CONSISTENCY

L
Z

Published by Learning Zone, LLC, an imprint of Brisance Books Group LLC.

Power Mental Golf® is a registered trademark of Learning Zone, LLC.

Learning Zone, LLC
3219 E Camelback Road, #355
Phoenix, AZ 85018
602 315-9700
Visit our Web site: PowerMentalGolf.com

Special Sales and Speaking Opportunities:
Contact Kerry Graham at KGraham@PowerMentalGolf.com

Printed in the United States of America
First Edition: June 2016
ISBN: 978-1-944194-08-6

062016

DEDICATION

To every golfer who has been touched by the joy in golf
and would like to have more of that joy.

ACKNOWLEDGMENTS

My ability to deliver this book is the result of a lifetime of support and help from so many great people. I have learned from and loved all these special mentors and friends. I also have learned from all of my students. From the day that I gave my first golf lesson, I have always known that each of my students would be my teacher and that has truly been the case. To all my family, friends, mentors, colleagues and students, I extend my deeply heartfelt appreciation.

Special thanks to my heaven-based best friends: my parents, Nancy and Bob, my brother Michael, and my husband Bill.

My very special thanks go to all my friends and family who have done so much to help me feel loved and appreciated. My sister Patricia and her husband Tim are the BEST! Their son, Navy Lieutenant Brandt Zykan, has been one of my best teachers on how to learn, laugh, and celebrate golf. Mona Gambetta has guided and encouraged me for years on all writing and expressing the issues of truth. Chuck Hogan was my first mentor in the breakthrough thinking of how we play golf internally to guide the physical. He set me on my journey for which I am so grateful. Thanks to my long time friends Lynn Marriott and Ben Crenshaw for their support. Thanks to Daffodil Sanchez, Jacquie LeMarr, Kelly Mahoney, and John Esslinger for digital and photo assistance. Special appreciation to Michael Murphy who has been my teacher throughout our instruction and then was so kind to be my advisor and editor of this book.

My best girlfriends and mentors are special in my heart and with gratitude I thank Cindy Sisson, Cindy Davis, Lyn St. James, and Linda Vollstedt.

Thanks to Ricki Linksman for believing in me as we joined on our journey to improve sharing knowledge of the incredible power of learning. And thanks to Gary Blaisdell who has walked the way with me on all these golf instruction and club fitting issues.

I so appreciate all my colleagues and friends at the Ladies Professional Golf Association. The LPGA supported my journey and gave me incredible leadership opportunities, for which I am very grateful.

As a child I became intrigued with learning and how each person learns so differently. My brother Michael had a Mensa IQ, but failed in the school education system. From a young age, because of the pain of his experience, I decided that in my lifetime I would find ways to learn as much as possible about how individuals learn. I found mentors and studied research and worked to apply that learning to my life and to my golf teaching.

For the past 30 years I have worked to apply everything I could learn about learning and teaching to help my students in their learning and love of the game of golf. I believe that every golf instructor has the responsibility to instill a sense of *self-esteem* in his or her students. I found that understanding a student's learning preference and guiding each to own his or her unique gifts enhances a student's *self-esteem* and helps each play their best golf.

I believe that a golf instructor should learn to understand the learning traits of each of their golf students and then match their teaching style to the student's learning style. But in order to do that there is an education process that's necessary for the teacher to learn how to identify learning preferences and how to adapt golf instruction to those preferences. When the instructor takes the time to learn this and apply it in his or her lessons, the student learns faster and more effectively.

I struggled with how to present all this information. I am always learning and know that all of this is a learning experience. I have been writing this book for over a year and as I expected, it has been an incredible learning experience. During this last year, my golf clients have either validated the information in this book or have shown me that there is more to learn. And I thank them for their testimonials and the case studies you'll find in this book.

The Power of Mental Golf is an offering to the improvement and future of golf teaching. I look forward to the feedback and to the evolution of ideas that will be used to take golf teaching to an even higher level.

CONTENTS

FOREWORD

I have known Kerry Graham for 25 years.

During that time I have learned from her and watched her leadership in golf. I have admired her steadfast curiosity for understanding how human beings learn and applying that learning to growing the game of golf.

Kerry has courageously taken a stand for better golf teaching her entire career. She has influenced the teachers in golf to move to a more student-centered approach to teaching and to value the importance of understanding learning styles and club fitting.

What Kerry has been advocating for decades worked long before we had the neuroscience to prove it. She saw it in the students she taught and the success they had playing better golf and enjoying it more.

We are blessed to now have cutting edge neuroscience to help us better understand what is going on in the brain when a student is learning golf and playing the game.

In *The Power of Mental Golf*, Kerry is helping us to use science and make it practical and applicable to the game of golf.

Lynn Marriott
VISION54

PREFACE

Sharing the journey of golf, our struggles, joys and dreams is a fun part of golf camaraderie.

Writing this book has been that kind of journey for me. I struggled, never wanted to quit, and wanted to be your best friend in delivering information that would help bring more golf joy to you.

The goal of my writing was to give inspiration and information to golfers and to blend the mental with the physical training and actual playing of golf. For me, that has been my goal as an instructor.

When I was close to finishing this book, I read a press release that changed the destiny of both the book and my journey. The press release announced a new technology that seemed to be able to validate the teaching methods I have advocated for decades. Upon investigation, I learned that it was true. A person could put on a head band and find out if they were "In the Zone." I purchased five of the headbands and did four months of research with my students to validate what they had been working on. The results were incredible and I added those case studies to this book.

The Power of Mental Golf will guide you to play golf with a singular focus—based on your brain processing strengths—and help create the "In the Zone" experience, better golf shots, and more fun. The new headband technology will validate that state and help you train to move "Into the Zone"—at will.

I wish you increased joy as you pursue your golf dreams.

INTRODUCTION

Welcome to a Learning Journey—about yourself and about your golf game.

Everyone plays golf for their own reasons. This book can assist *you* in accomplishing your goals to learn more about how and why you play and enjoy the great game of golf.

A little about me... and how I entered the game of golf and how I have become so passionate about golf instruction and learning more about the mental aspects of golf.

I began playing golf with my family when I was nine years old and played junior competitive golf in Wyoming and intercollegiate varsity golf at Arizona State University.

My golf-teaching journey began in 1971; it was my first job out of college. I immediately loved the interactions with each student and being able to contribute to their lives through golf. I was eager to learn how to teach well so I read all the books and attended as many seminars on teaching the game that were available anywhere in the country. I was married to a PGA Tour Professional and traveled on the PGA Tour with him in the 1970s. Those were the early great tour days for Jack Nicklaus, Arnold Palmer, Gary Player, Lee Trevino, and so many other icons of the game. I watched them play and practice and learned from them and their teachers. We were living in Phoenix, Arizona, where I taught golf when not traveling on the PGA Tour and applied all I was learning. That was truly a magic time for golf and for me.

I settled down in Phoenix in 1980 and dedicated all my efforts to teaching golf. I also returned to my studies at Arizona State University and earned a Master's Degree in Learning Psychology. My golf teaching continued to progress, but I always sensed that there was more I could learn to be a better teacher.

I was elected National President of the LPGA Teaching Division in 1987. My intent was to find better resources for golf instruction and instructor training. The next six years were life changing for me and for my golf instruction. I had support from the LPGA through those years to found the LPGA-USGA Girls Golf Club, the LPGA Urban Youth Golf Program, and the Women's Golf Summits. They all made an impact in changing the face of golf. It was during those years that I began a new journey to understand how we learn and how we could be better instructors.

I am writing this book to offer a different approach and perspective for each golfer and each golf instructor who reads it and may suspect that there is something missing in their learning/teaching tools and results.

Learning and adapting THE POWER OF MENTAL GOLF (PMG) FIVE-PART SYSTEM to your game will bring you to a whole new place with your golf game. This book will be your guide:

PART I
Get to Know Your Brain

PART II
Golf Shot Routine

PART III
Habits Produce Consistency

PART IV
Golf Equipment Needs to Fit

PART V
New Computer Technology Validates Your Mental Management

PART I   Get to Know Your Brain

Everyone has unique and individual brain processing systems. The future of great school education will be to identify each student's brain processing systems at the time of entry to elementary school. When this is done, the students will then matriculate through their entire education knowing "how" they best learn. That will require the education system and all the teachers to be aware of their own learning biases and adjust their teaching to fit the preferences of the students.

Today, few children or adults know their learning preferences. To learn how to play your best golf with confidence and consistency, you will want to know your learning preferences and use those to create focus when you practice and play. A revolution in the golf teaching industry will occur when golf instructors begin to base their teaching on their students' unique learning preferences.

My first goal as a teacher is to understand how I process information and then how my students process information. I can then better guide them to manage those processes when learning and playing golf. It is also my goal as a teacher to present all information to them *in their preferred learning style.*

What is your preferred learning style and brain processing preference? How can you know your students' preferences? Chapter 1, Get to Know Your Brain, provides this information.

PART II   Golf Shot Routine

There is a simple and repetitive mental brain/body function that guides the body to move automatically to hit the ball like you tie your shoes, type, ride a bike, or park your car. Once you repeat an action over and over, it becomes a memory and the body can move automatically.

Many golf teachers and books talk about the "Pre-Shot Routine," suggesting that a golfer should rehearse and repeat the same actions before executing the golf shot. What you will learn in Chapter 2 is that a "Pre-

Shot Routine" is *not* enough. Instead, the "Golf Shot Routine" is what a golfer should learn and use for success.

The "Golf Shot Routine" includes the entire process of each golf shot—before, during, and after the shot—and defining both one's physical and mental processes.

Each complete shot takes only one to three minutes. The golf swing takes less than two seconds. To play consistent golf you will want to establish a unique and successful mental and physical process for those minutes and make it a habit!

Most golfers use random pre-shot routines—different every time with resulting random and inconsistent results. Once you establish your personal and unique "Golf Shot Routine" your confidence and consistency will increase substantially.

Chapter 2—Golf Shot Routine—will guide you to design your unique routine.

PART III Habits Produce Consistency

Neuroscientific research is taking us to a whole new place!!! Hold on—it's a wild ride!

Modern brain research has finally proved many things humans have always suspected.

Scientists can now observe and measure the way the brain's various elements work including the electromagnetic flow of energy through the body and out of the body from our thoughts. Our thoughts generate energy and affect our bodies and the universe around us.

Research has discovered that the heart and the stomach have brains that interact on a constant energy flow with the cranial brain and proved that the "brain" in the heart has neuron strength equal to the cranial brain!

Organizing our thoughts can change our golf and our life! It's not just a hope and a dream any more. Scientists have discovered through brain research why you can tie your shoes successfully *every time* without thinking about it, and why hitting consistent golf shots should be much easier if we use our brain in the proper way.

Habits are formed in the brain and allow the body to flow in movement and action repetitively with high levels of consistency. Forming the simple and correct personal habits can help the golfer create a golf swing that is automatic and allow them to be "In the Zone" in practice and play. Myelination is a medical term that refers to the process of forming memory and habits in the brain. Around the axon paths in your brain is a myelin sheath (a layer of myelin) that helps increase the speed at which information can travel between the neurons. Myelinating the golf shot approach, golf swing and golf skills by doing precise repetitions of what you want will lead to higher consistency and confidence.

Chapter 3 will describe the advantages of myelinating the golf shot approach and swing.

PART IV   Golf Equipment Needs to Fit

One of the contributing factors to confidence and consistency rests in the golf equipment you are using. The better your equipment is fit to your learning style, body design, and strength, the better your learning and playing will be. With misfit equipment, your brain will have to change your natural swing to create consistency. The golfer will always be trying to create compensations to make the ball go where he or she wants it to go. Compensations are very difficult to repeat when the pressure is on. The body wants to make a natural athletic motion and compensations are not the most natural, athletic motions. With a golf swing that takes less than two seconds, it is difficult, if not impossible, to make those compensations consistently. Even if you practice them they will often disappear when under pressure.

A substantial percentage of golf equipment being used by many amateur golfers and some professionals is not matched to them, to their learning styles, body height, body proportions, and to their strength.

Consider other things you do in your life that require that you match the product to your individual body style and/or strength:

- Adjustment of your car seat and for professional drivers, custom-fitted seats.
- Snow skis and boots are carefully fitted, with liability factors if the fit is wrong.
- Your clothing is purchased to fit your body proportions.
- Weight Training is all adjusted for your body proportions and strength.
- Bowling balls are selected based on your finger size and strength.
- Wedding rings are selected based on your finger size.

Look at this list. Consider what would happen if there were no fitting or very random and limited fitting available in any of those categories—not pretty!

The problem is that the golf industry has not figured out how to tell you the truth about how important club fitting is and is not providing excellence in club fitting for you. In Chapter 4, you will learn the history of golf equipment and club fitting and what you can do to better understand golf equipment to ensure that your equipment matches you and enhances your game.

I have been involved in the club fitting of thousands of golfers. In many cases, when students finally get to hit with a club that is a better fit for them, their ball striking ability soars, along with their confidence and consistency. It is fascinating to see that most golfers with misfit clubs suspect that there might be something wrong with their clubs and have that belief upheld when they hit a club better matched to them. While improper club fitting exists in all categories of the game, it is especially inadequate for tall men and women, the entire women's category, and juniors.

Chapter 4 is a guide for you to get your Golf Equipment Fit for You.

**PART V   New Computer Technology—Mental and Medical—
Validate Your Ability to Manage Your Brain**

If you can consistently improve your mental game and stay healthy, you can play better golf now and create something that can be a lifetime enjoyment. In Chapter 5, I share with you the leading-edge technologies for improving your mental game and assisting your golf health. Amazing new products are available to help you stay at the top of your game.

The first five chapters of this book define the PMG System. Now: How do you coach?

CHAPTER 6   You Are Your Best Coach

Chapter 6 is for you, the golfer. While it is good to have a guide, instructor, or coach, you ultimately are your own coach when learning, practicing, and playing golf. How efficient are you as your own coach?

Every golfer is a Player and at the same time, their own Coach. When you are practicing and playing, you will often talk to yourself about your expectations, your swing, the shot results, and plans for improving, etc. You make constant judgments about your shot results, performance, feedback, reactions, and adjustments. How well are you coaching yourself? Are you a nurturing, caring Coach, or are you tough and mean to you, the Player? Do you keep it simple or do you overwhelm you, the Player, with too much information? You cannot avoid being your own Coach, but you have the opportunity to make a choice about the kind of Coach you want to be. Just think for a moment about the way you talk to yourself on the range and on the course. Is it usually pretty harsh, especially at times when your performance does not meet your expectations?

When I am introducing a physical change to a golf student, I ask them to practice it *away* from the golf ball. Research has proven that repetitions for 15 to 20 minutes a day, every day, for a few weeks will solidify the physical change so that it becomes a habit. But if you are hitting balls when trying to make the change a habit, it won't work as effectively. You must give your complete attention to a physical change as you practice to make it a habit. Once it is habit, it will be automatic for you. Then you can put your complete focus on the shot, using your sensory cues to put you "In the Zone." You will need to be Your Best Coach to do the repetition work away from the golf ball.

Chapter 6, You Are Your Best Coach, will guide you to apply the concepts in this book to learn to coach yourself with excellence while practicing and playing. You will also be guided on how to share this information with your golf instructor to better assist you on this journey.

CHAPTER 7 Be One of the Best Instructors
Whether you are a professional golf instructor, a school golf coach, a kids' coach in the local junior golf program, or a golf coach for your family or friends, this information can be extremely helpful. This chapter will help you organize the information in this book along with other best practices in golf instruction and give you a way to assess what information and tools you might want to add to your instruction protocols.

Chapter 7, Be One of the Best Instructors, speaks to the golf instructor.

CHAPTER 8 Learning with the Tour Pros
The Tour Professionals are elite athletes with incredible talents. When we watch them play and win, we should be inspired. It is important to recognize that they are dealing with all the same struggles every golfer faces—the pressure to perform and equipment fitting issues.

In Chapter 8, Learning with the Tour Pros, you will be offered insight to watching golf professionals and learning with them.

CHAPTER 9 But... What About Swing Mechanics?
Integrating the learning of physical golf skills - golf swing and short game skills - with learning the mental game is the real mark of excellence in golf instruction.

CHAPTER 1

GET TO KNOW YOUR BRAIN

Everyone has unique and individual brain processing systems. The future of great education will be to identify each student's brain processing systems at the time of entry to school. The students will matriculate through their entire education knowing "how" they best learn. That will require the education system and all their teachers to be aware of their own learning biases and adjust their teaching to fit the preferences of the students. That will also make it easier for people to learn activities like golf.

To learn and play your best golf, it will be to your advantage to know your learning preferences. If you are working with a golf instructor, share your learning preferences and ask your instructor to present the information in the ways you best learn.

Every time I work with a golf student, my goal as a golf instructor is to understand how my student processes information to learn and perform, and then to guide them to manage those processes when learning and playing golf. It is also my goal as an instructor to present all information to them *in their preferred learning style.*

My favorite resource to help my students identify their learning preferences is based on the work of Ricki Linksman, an educator, author, and speaker from Illinois. Her best-known book is *How to Learn Anything Quickly! Quick, Easy Tips to Improve Memory, Reading Comprehension, and Test-Taking Skills through the Brain's Fastest Superlinks Learning Style*, (National Reading Diagnostics Institute, 1996-2015).

Her life's work has been to write and administer her Superlinks to Accelerated Learning System™* that gives the individual a fast and easy way to determine how they most quickly and naturally learn and process information. I have been using Ricki's work for over 15 years to help me better understand how each of my golf clients uniquely learns and processes information. Ricki has agreed to share the information from her practice, books, and websites to help the readers of this book.

As a golf instructor, the most common questions my students ask are:

"How can I learn golf faster and easier?"

"How can I be more confident?"

"Why am I not consistent? I occasionally hit a good shot—why can't I do it all the time?"

"What should I think about before I hit a shot?"

"What should I think while I am hitting the ball?"

"How do I take the confidence I feel on the practice range to the course?"

For many years, I struggled to answer those questions. I earned a Master's Degree in Learning Psychology and studied Sports Psychology, but still didn't know those answers. Now, with the information provided by brain research in the last 10 years and with the tools that Ricki Linksman has provided, the answers are more available. The goal in this book will be to provide you a better understanding of *how your brain* uniquely processes information and to guide you in using that personal information to better *manage your brain*.

Let's get started!

---

* © Copyright 1993-2016 by Ricki Linksman, National Reading Diagnostics Institute

STEP ONE: Take The Learning Assessment

1. Go to the PMG Website: www.powermentalgolf.com

2. Click on Learning Assessment Info on the Home page.

3. Use the Code PMG18 to receive a special discount offer for book owners. With that code you will be offered substantial discounts on single and multiple Learning Assessments.

4. Follow the instructions to link directly to the Learning Assessment.

5. After you complete the Assessment you will get the results that you can print. Use that information about your learning preferences as you read the rest of this chapter and book.

Using your Learning Assessment result, fill in your unique information below:

My Sensory System Strengths:

1. _____

2. _____
    (If secondary is given in test results.)

My Brain Processing Preferences:

LEFT_____   or RIGHT_____   or BOTH _____

For you as a golfer, these preferences come into play consistently in the following experiences:

- Learning a new swing skill
- Learning to read greens
- Best practice methods
- Staying focused during practice

- Taking your range game to the course
- Exactly how to focus in practice and on the course
- How to identify personal cues within your learning system
- How to calm your mind and get "Into the Zone"

Within each learning category, individuals will be different. Use your imagination and your experience to discover your cues and understanding how you can explore using your personal strengths in a simple way for learning, practice, and play.

STEP TWO: Apply the Golfer's Guide

This step matches your Sensory Strengths and Brain Processing Preferences with your Golf Learning Type(s). In the next section you'll find the Golfer's Guide to Brain Management—in text and as a chart.

Golfer's Guide to Brain Management

Below are the Learning Style types that combine the preferred sensory system with the preference of left or right brain. Included for each Style are the learning preferences, the type of cues each prefers, and the weaknesses of each type that could interfere with success in learning and performing for each type.

VISUAL LEFT (V-L)

To learn the golf swing or short game, a V-L person prefers to use visual guides—pictures, books, power points, and mirrors. V-Ls like to break things down into detail and then put it all together. The cue for the V-L person will be an image. The image could be anything visual and is unique for each individual. An example of singular visual images includes focusing on the target, or on an image beyond the target on the target line, or an image of the finish position. The weaknesses to learn to manage are the tendency to think and move very fast, especially under pressure. It is also easy for too many images to come to mind as the V-L person is getting ready and executing the golf shot. Taking too much time over the ball may give time for too many images to flow in. Being prepared and committed to the single cue before getting over the ball will keep the execution time to a minimum. Talking to oneself over the ball will easily cause distraction. Sticking to an image cue rather than words will provide better execution.

VISUAL RIGHT (V-R)

To learn the golf swing or short game, a V-R person prefers to use colored pictures, illustrations, powerpoints, videos, and DVDs. V-Rs like to focus first on the whole swing or shot image and then break it down if needed. They like to see everything as a whole. The V-R person will have a single cue and it will be a visual image, often in color, though it could be still or full motion. The image could be anything visual and is unique for each individual. Example: singular images are an image of the whole swing motion, of the target, the swing position, or the ball flight path. The weaknesses to learn to manage are the tendency to think and move very fast, especially under pressure. It is also easy for too many images to come to mind as they are getting ready and executing the golf shot. Taking too much time over the ball may allow time for multiple images to flow in. Being prepared and committed to the single cue before getting over the ball will keep the execution time to a minimum. Talking to oneself over the ball will easily cause distraction. Sticking to an image cue rather than words will provide better execution.

AUDITORY LEFT (A-L)

To learn the golf swing or short game, an A-L person prefers verbal instruction, with detail. A-Ls like to record the instruction or use video with auditory guidance. They like sequential learning and like to discuss and get confirmation with verbal feedback. Cues for the A-L person will be associated with instructional words or a phrase. It will be a single cue. The cue could be anything auditory and is unique for each individual. Example singular auditory cues are words with movement or just words.

The instructor should encourage A-L students to dialogue with each other about the swing and movements. One weakness is the tendency to have negative and critical self-talk.

AUDITORY RIGHT (A-R)

To learn the golf swing or short game, the A-R person prefers to observe the swing or motion of the short game by demonstration or video with sound effects or short, action words. The instructor should use few key words. They may want to record the video with music or sound effects, or voiceover instructions for later review. Cues for the A-R person will be auditory, based in sounds and music. It will be a single verbal or sound effect cue used on each shot. The verbal phrase or sound could be anything and is unique for each individual. Examples of singular A-R cues are whistling, humming, or making sound effects to sense rhythm. A-R people like sound and key words. The weaknesses to learn to manage are the tendency to have distracting inner talk or reacting negatively to too many words in the verbal directions.

TACTILE LEFT (T-L)

To learn the golf swing or short game, the T-L person prefers to feel the swing or motion of the short game by guided demonstration by the instructor or video. Cues for the T-L person will be a single feeling cue used on each shot. The feeling image could be anything and is unique for each individual, often based in feeling peaceful and calm when hitting their shots. Examples of singular T-L images are feelings of motion like sweeping the floors with a broom. The T-L likes to write the instruction during or after the instruction session. Writing the instruction helps them learn. The T-L person thrives with positive reinforcement such as positive facial expressions, tone of voice, and body language. The weaknesses to learn to manage are the tendency to have distracting, negative, and self-critical inner talk and feeling uncomfortable with the instructor or other students.

TACTILE RIGHT (T-R)

To learn the golf swing or short game, the T-R person prefers to take notes in color, draw sketches, watch the instructor modeling the moves, and view pictures or sketches in books and magazines. They prefer to first view the whole swing demonstrated by the instructor or a video and then break it into parts and details. They can learn with or without music. They like being outdoors and using their hands. They learn best when they feel liked by the instructor and other students. Cues for the T-R person are based in feeling peaceful and calm when hitting their shots. They do well with a cue that creates their peaceful internal place. That could be a memory of their favorite peaceful places, experiences, or images, like the beach, mountains, peaceful friendships, etc. T-R cues will be based in their heart and hands working together and they will do well to have their favorites—clothes, glove, ball, etc. They will have higher personal peace and success when they play with people they like and with an instructor they feel comfortable with. Their cue will be a singular tactile sensation involving having feeling or sense of touch that will put them in the zone by feeling peaceful. The weaknesses to learn to manage are the tendency to be sensitive to negative feelings from people on the course or from the instructor. They will be sensitive to situations that interfere with their physical comfort like clothes that are too tight, being too hot or cold, negative people, etc.

KINESTHETIC LEFT (K-L)

To learn the golf swing or short game, the K-L person prefers to use large muscles. They like to view demonstrations or video and move along with them while they are watching, and can tie these to verbal directions. They like organized, sequential details with key action words while in motion. They thrive on competition in learning and in tracking improvement. The K-L person likes comfortable clothing for freedom to move. Cues for the K-L person are based in feeling the motion of the swing in their large muscles and feeling the connection of their feet to the earth. They may have unique cues that focus on a particular position or motion in the swing. Many K-Ls like to cue on the sense of large motion movement and perhaps find it smooth, slow, light, in the groove, etc. The weaknesses to learn to manage are the tendency to have tension and therefore restricted motion. They often can have tension and not be aware of it. Talking or listening too much when they are playing or practicing distracts from their natural motion. Breathing and practicing awareness of tension in their body is important. Due to their need to win, avoid the tendency to quit or give up or shut down if a mistake is made. Accept that mistakes are positive steps in the learning process.

KINESTHETIC RIGHT (K-R)

To learn the golf swing or short game, the K-R person prefers to view the whole swing or short game motion by demonstration of the instructor or by video with a few key action words of explanation. The K-R person likes nonverbal instruction and staying in motion while learning. They like competition and winning in games and they like tracking improvement. They can choose to use music or no music when learning. They like to be shown the motions and then they want to do them. Cues for the K-R person are based in creating muscle relaxation in the body. It is helpful for the K-R golfer to identify where the stress in the body is most likely to create tension. The cues can be a particular large muscle sensation in a position or motion and often focus on the sense of large motion movement and sensing for instance, the smooth, easy, light sense of that movement. They may sense the groove coming into the hit, or some part of the physical motion through the hit. The weaknesses the K-R needs to learn to manage are the tendencies to allow tension to arise in the body, especially as the pressure increases. Talking or listening too much when practicing or playing can be very distracting from the physical focus necessary to stay in relaxation. Breathing and shaking out the hands are helpful to reduce the tension, in practice and playing. Due to their need to win, they need to avoid the tendency to quit or give up or shut down if a mistake is made. Accept that mistakes are positive steps in the learning process.

Golfer's Guide to Brain Management

	PREFERRED LEARNING METHODS	CUES	AVOID WEAKNESSES
V-L **Visual** **Left**	Use Visual guides - pictures, books, powerpoints, mirrors; can break down into detail. Likes sequential learning.	Single visual image or target, finish.	Think and move too fast. Create too many images over ball. Too much inner talk.
V-R **Visual** **Right**	Use colored pictures, illustrations, videos, powerpoints, DVDs; focus on whole swing or shot image first, before breaking down into step by step.	Single visual image in color of whole motion, target, or swing position.	Think and move too fast. Create too many images over ball. Too much inner talk.
A-L **Auditory** **Left**	Likes verbal instruction, with detail. Can tape record or use video with auditory guidance. Likes sequential learning and likes to discuss and get confirmation with verbal feedback.	Single cue consisting of a word, words, or a phrase.	Too much inner talk. Too much negative inner critical talk.
A-R **Auditory** **Right**	Observe swing or motion by demo or video with sound effects, music, or short action key words. Instructor should use few words. Tape record the instruction with music or sound effects or short key action words.	Whistling, humming, word or phrase with sound effects or music.	Too fast. Too much inner talk. Too much verbal direction.
T-L **Tactile** **Left**	Write notes to confirm instruction. Sequential, step by step, outlines of learning materials. Likes positive feelings, instructors and players. Verbal or written feedback from Instructor.	Single feeling cue involving hands and feelings or sense of touch. Create a peaceful place and maintain through execution. Feelings of swing. Likes using hands.	Negativity of others, negative tone of voice, facial expressions, body language. Negative situations that cause physical discomfort.
T-R **Tactile** **Right**	Draws sketches, takes notes, or views pictures or sketches in books and magazines. View whole swing as demo or in video first and then break into details. Can choose to learn with or without music. Likes being outdoors, using hands. Learns when instructor and others are liked.	Feeling cue involving hands, feelings, or sense of touch. Create sense of a peaceful internal place. Hands and Heart work together. Use favorites - clothes, glove, ball, etc. Play with others you like and select an Instructor you like.	Negative sense of instructor or other players in group by negative tone of voice, facial expressions, body language. Over sensitive about pleasing others. Often concerned about creating stress for others instead of focusing on golf shot.

9

	PREFERRED LEARNING METHODS	CUES	AVOID WEAKNESSES
K-L **Kinesthetic** **Left**	Likes using large motor muscles to learn. Views demo or video and moves with it and verbal direction with key action words. Likes organized, sequential details while in motion. Likes competition in learning and tracking improvement. Likes comfortable clothing for freedom to move.	Relaxation in Body. Feeling motion of swing in their large muscles. Likes feel of feet connected to earth. Likes cues involving particular position or motion and cues that capture sense of large motion movement, i.e. smooth.	Tension and restricted motion. Talking or listening too much distracts from motion. Due to need to win, avoid giving up, quitting, or shutting down if a mistake is made. Learn that mistakes are positive steps in the learning process.
K-R **Kinesthetic** **Right**	Views whole swing by demo or video with a few key action words of explanation. Like nonverbal instruction. Likes staying in motion while learning. Likes competition and games in learning and tracking improvement. Can choose to use music or no music.	Relaxation in body. Identify areas where most stress tends to occur. Cue can be a particular position or motion or cues that capture sense of large motion movement i.e. smooth.	Tension and restricted motion. Talking or listening too much distracts from motion. Due to need to win, avoid getting frustrated, quitting, giving up or shutting down if a mistake is made. Learn that mistakes are positive steps in the learning process.

STEP THREE: Get Into the Zone — Identify Your Favorite Cues

What Is It Like to Be "In the Zone?"

We all have had the experience of doing something in our lives when, on a given day or for a period of time, it just seemed so easy to perform. Athletes have often described this experience of success as:

> "The basket looked as big as a peach barrel."

> "The golf hole looked three times bigger than normal."

> "I could see the line on the green as if it had been drawn with a magic marker."

> "The spot to hit the serve on the tennis court was huge and colored."

> "When I threw the winning pass, I saw a big black circle in the sky and threw the ball through the circle."

> "It seemed like time stood still."

> "It was just so easy."

"I just knew I could do it—I didn't think about it and there was no doubt that it would work."

"I visualized the golf shot and it did exactly what I visualized."

These experiences happen in sports and can happen in all aspects of our life, when we are "present in the moment" and our body and brain are totally in sync, resulting in our best performance. Time flies and this is a time when we are most creative.

The sports industry has labeled this experience as being "In the Zone." Whenever you see an especially successful sports experience, you can be assured that the athlete was "In the Zone."

Athletes can get "In the Zone" when they are "present in the moment," stop telling their body what to do, and get in sync with their target through the strength of their sensory system preferences. For instance, Visuals see and act. Auditories sense their private rhythm or balance, and tell themselves what to do and how to act. Tactiles pre-feel the movement in their hands and their feelings and perform well when in a peaceful state. Kinesthetics feel their large motor muscles and like to sense specific muscle relaxation.

We have six active sensory systems: Visual, Auditory, Tactile, Kinesthetic, Gustatory, and Olfactory. It is through our sensory systems that we know or sense our world. If we did not have these sensory systems connecting our brain to our bodily functions, we would not know the world. It is through the strength of the various sensory systems that we play sports, choose activities that satisfy the needs of our sensory connections, and find our place in the world.

Exercise to Discover Your Favorite Cues for Performance
During my instruction time I guide my clients through the following experience. I encourage you to guide yourself through this experience and let me know if you need help.

Warm up at the range. After warming up, take your favorite club and just begin to hit shots. Don't think about swing mechanics and just hit shots. Begin to evaluate each shot with a number from 10 (excellent) to 1 (not acceptable). Base your evaluation on "how you generally like the shot." Don't try to change or fix your swing—*just continue hitting balls* at a nice calm pace.

After you hit a shot that you evaluate at 7 or above, stop and ask yourself, "How was that experience different?" The answer you are looking for is in a singular focus you had before and/or as you hit. For Visuals it will probably be a picture, for Auditories it will probably be a word, sound effect, music, or a sense of rhythm or balance, for Tactiles it will probably be a feeling or sensation in the hands and a sense of peace and calm, and for Kinesthetics, it will probably be a muscular sensation in the swing or set up or finish.

This will begin an exploration of what singular cue helps you connect through your sensory system with your target and releases your attempt to control your swing. It may be difficult in the beginning to identify the single sensory cue you had before you hit your best shots. If the cue is not obvious, stay quiet, relaxed and continue hitting, and evaluating each shot with the number system, asking yourself how it was different when you evaluate the shot at 7 or above.

When you think you have identified a cue, go ahead and use it as a singular cue to hit some shots. If you hit good shots, it's a good cue for you. If you are being clear on the singular cue, but still don't hit good shots, let that cue go and continue to explore for a different singular cue or image within your sensory preference that can bring you success. Be patient. This is a journey. I have led many golfers of all levels to find their favorite cues. Some can identify it right away and others need more time on the journey to discover their magic cue and family of cues. Because all this sensory awareness is new to our perceptions about golf and life, it may take a while for you to be aware of your sensory strengths and images. I cannot teach my clients what their cues are, but rather I can lead them by questions to bring their awareness to their cues when they have success. From there, they can become aware of what their thoughts and images are when they are *not* having success.

Examples of Favorite Cues

Below are examples of unique personal cues that golfers have discovered within certain brain processing styles. These are simply examples, and you will have a unique cue based on *your* processing systems. Here are some examples to get you started on your journey.

Visual:

- Visualize a target—a precise point in the distance or a general image, such as a tree or something on the target line.
- Hold follow-through position, with an image of yourself in your follow through.
- Visualize an image of your full swing, like a movie.
- Visualize an image of the club going through contact, like a movie.
- Focus on seeing a spot on the ball or the back of the ball.
- Imagine a target (of any description) in the horizon and shoot toward the image.
- Imagine the ball flight as a line in the sky, sometimes in color.
- Imagine a line of any color on the putting green, from the ball into the hole.

Auditory:

- Sense a particular rhythm to the swing, identified by a counting or a cadence or a tune or perhaps a number for the speed of the swing (1 – 10).
- Sense a music score in the target area and hit toward the music.
- Sense a precise pause at the top of the backswing.

Tactile:

- Imagine your favorite peaceful place i.e. beach, ocean, spa.
- Use your mantra from meditation.

- Breathe and clear your mind of thoughts.
- Sense the best feeling of the grip, like a handshake.

Kinesthetic:
- Relaxation of arms and hands
- Internal relaxation that creates a go signal once the relaxation is felt
- A certain feeling in the set-up, swing or follow-through that can be sensed and felt in a large motor muscle or group every time the shot is good
- Smooth, flowing
- Imagine the joy of being a winner

These are examples that give you an idea of how to explore your sensory imaging process. The cues that will be best for you will be yours personally: one(s) that will put you at ease and allow you to swing fully and freely. Everyone is unique and your personal cue will be unique to your sensory system, your brain processing preferences, and your life experiences. Once you discover your favorite cue(s), you will increase in consistency and confidence in shots. Not every shot will be exceptional, but in general the shots will be more consistent.

When you sense a cue that might be a favorite, use that single cue hitting three balls. If the cue is a good one for you, your ball striking will become more confident and consistent. If you do not find increased consistency within striking three to four balls, that cue is not a good one for you. Then, look for a different cue.

The cues that each player finds most efficient will be within the range of Sensory System strengths for that individual. Refer to the Golfer's Guide list of Cue suggestions for guidance.

MOST IMPORTANT:
When hitting shots, chips or putts, commit to a single cue.

Use only a single cue, whether it's a word, image, feeling, sense of rhythm, etc. Commit to a single cue and then use only that single cue over the ball. If you are distracted by an external distraction, i.e. a noise or movement, or internally distracted by other cues, thoughts, or images that may enter into your mind as you stand over the ball, back off, commit to the single cue and move back in to execute the shot with that single cue.

With knowledge of your learning preferences and the sensory cue examples in this book, work to identify your favorite and most natural cues. Then use the single cue technique when practicing and playing. Make committing to and using a single cue a habit. Brain research confirms that the normal function of the brain is to think many thoughts all the time. For problem solving and multi-tasking in life, that works. But for hitting golf shots, the function of thinking many thoughts over the ball defeats the ability of the body to create a natural, free flowing, swing. Thinking all those thoughts interferes with the brain's ability to send clear messages to the body to produce the swing that is in the memory.

Have you ever wondered why, when you get so frustrated and give up telling your body what to do to make a golf swing, it is then that you usually hit your best shots? Finally, out of frustration you give it up—you stop directing your swing mechanics and it is then that you often hit a good shot. Then you say, "How did that happen? Why can't I do that all the time?" You will hit good shots more often if you follow the guides in this book. Most people allow their brains to use many thoughts or images over the golf ball and doing that becomes a bad habit. Processing more than one thought or image becomes a distraction. Having numerous thoughts over the ball makes it very difficult to get "In the Zone."

To get started on a better path, practice using *only one cue—one thought or image for each shot.* Make it a habit and rely on the Single Cue Technique under pressure. Commit to that single cue before you walk into the shot. Keep that cue singular and execute the shot.

STEP FOUR: Create your Golf Shot Routine

In Chapter 2, you will learn the Golf Shot Routine that will help you integrate your Single Cue into your Golf Shot Routine. This will create a habit of making your preparation, execution, and finishing your golf shot. Your Golf Shot Routine will provide you the way to make your golf consistent.

Finding a Matching Golf Instructor

In trying to find a teaching professional who will appreciate your learning preferences, you should ask yourself the following questions:

- Who was your favorite teacher—in school or other life endeavors?
- How did that teacher present materials and impact how you learned?
- How do the cues from your Learning Preferences fit this experience?
- Have you had a golf teacher who fits this profile?

If you are already working with a golf teacher that you like and with whom you are having success, share this book and information, and spend time explaining to your golf teacher how you best learn.

CHAPTER 2

GOLF SHOT ROUTINE

"How do I improve my Mental Game?" All golfers—professionals and amateurs, as well as golf television broadcasters—are in quest of that answer. Most golfers believe that if they hit a poor shot they have made a "swing error" and go to the next shot(s) trying to fix their last swing error in order to hit a better shot. Doesn't that sound familiar?

But at some point all golfers think or say one or more of the following:

"That was a mental error."

"My game is between my ears."

"My brain is so messed up."

Then they show up on lesson tees around the world asking teaching professionals to help them make their game better. What they really want to say, but often don't, is: "I think it's between my ears." Or "How do I make my mental game better?" And that is the main theme of this book.

When Jordan Spieth, Rory McIlroy, and Jason Day make great shots, the comments from the TV commentators usually focus on their swings:

"That was a great swing."

"That was great balance."

"BizHub shows us his perfect move through the ball."

Only occasionally will a TV commentator or a player in the press conference talk about FOCUS. The performances by Jordan, Rory, and

Jason on their winning days give the fans a sense that there is something more going on than thinking about their golf swing. Their golf swings vary from each other but, more importantly, the way they focus is unique and different.

In August of 2015, Jason Day, won the PGA Championship at Whistling Straights in Wisconsin. His victory was dominant and from the 1ˢᵗ tee to the 18ᵗʰ green, he gave the golf world an insight to *focus*. All the best players have simple cues they use to keep their brain quiet during execution. They usually don't talk about it, and because their cues are internal, the spectators don't know what they are doing. However, Jason Day gave some insight to all of us that day. Before every shot he stood behind the ball, closed his eyes, and visualized the shot. The TV commentators noticed and mentioned it often during his final round. What the commentators could not say was exactly how Jason was visualizing his shot. Only Jason knows that and he has become very good at it. Sometime in the previous year, Jason had learned how to get "In the Zone." His dominant win in the 2016 Player's Championship continues his journey of winning with great focus and being #1 player in the world. It has been very interesting to watch and obviously good for Jason. Every person finds his or her focus uniquely and that is Jason's way. What is yours?

Let's consider some important facts about golf and the human brain:

1. **Golf is a game of Action, not Reaction.** Tennis and baseball, for instance, are games of Reaction. In those sports, the ball is coming at you and you react to hit it. In golf, archery, and target shooting, the participant is in complete control of initiating when the action begins.

For golf, that is the secret to consistency—how to manage your brain to consistently initiate and repeat the action.

2. **The human brain is a problem-solving machine.** When a problem or opportunity presents itself to a person, the brain processes the problem with energy, chemicals, images, and feelings that have been labeled

"thoughts." The brain processes between 20,000 to 70,000 thoughts a day. There are 86,400 seconds in a 24-hour day. Therefore, the average brain is processing between one and four thoughts every four seconds. When the brain is taking in facts to analyze, organize, and make a decision, processing many thoughts can be productive. When you stand over a drive on the 18th hole, how many analyzing thoughts do you want to process? Do you hit better shots when you process fewer analyzing thoughts or more? The answer is that processing fewer thoughts or even a single thought (or in some cases, no thoughts) is the most productive mode.

What does your brain do when you are playing golf? Who is managing your brain?

Pick your favorite hole. Imagine walking up the fairway to your shot. As you approach the ball, you will begin the problem-solving process with many thoughts. Your brain will take in the pertinent information—including the lie, the wind, the conditions around the intended target, and the distance to the target. You will focus on your exact chosen target for this shot and then, with all that information, you will come to a decision and select a club. "Thanks Brain,"... that was a good problem-solving experience.

Now it is time to execute the shot. Is this "Problem Solving Time?" *No!* The swing takes less than two seconds. How many problem-solving "thoughts" do you want working on this task for those two seconds? How many thoughts do you use to create the "shoe-tying," "riding your bike," or "typing" experience? None or one. With practice, your golf swing and shot can have that same type of focus. With a singular focus, your golf swing can become a habit and you will be able to trust it. You trust your brain and your memory to send automatic messages to your body parts to execute those other actions. Your goal will be to trust your brain, and your memory to send the automatic messages to your body to produce the golf swing you have been practicing.

The problem for most golfers is that they don't move out of the Problem-Solving Brain Mode to hit the shot. Once they get over the ball they begin to trigger swing thoughts, emotional control thoughts, lists, and images. They do it because their multi-thinking has become a habit. They have not practiced a singular focus method and have emotional stress, or often think they need to tell their body what to do. However, those multiple thoughts interfere with the free-flowing golf swing that they can experience when they don't have many thoughts. Continue to read on in this chapter and book to find out how to discover how you uniquely focus your brain to execute your best and consistent shots, how you use the analytical left brain, and how you release into the right creative brain to execute the shot.

The brain is triggering thoughts all the time... that is how it is built for problem solving. It is not easy to maintain single focus with the brain. With years of meditation, some people can do that. Most golfers do not know that single focus is more productive for successful shots.

Many of my golf students through the years have asked me, "What should I think?" when hitting the shot. For many years I had to tell them that I didn't know. Brain research was not there yet. But now we know more about how the brain works and more about the body/brain connection, so I can guide you to figure out what you should think when hitting a golf shot.

GOLF SHOT ROUTINE

Instructors usually talk about the "Pre-Shot Routine." I recommend that the golf industry change that label to **"Golf Shot Routine."**

The **Golf Shot Routine** begins with the assessment, commitments, and then execution. The completion of the Golf Shot Routine is the Finish with a single Positive Thought. All those phases include mental and physical activity.

The emphasis for the Pre-Shot Routine is on the repetition of the physical habit of preparing before hitting the shot. The physical is an important part of this, but the missing piece in the Pre-Shot Routine that has to be added to be an integral part of the **Golf Shot Routine** is training the golfer to prepare and create the mental process before, during execution, and after the shot. The complete Golf Shot Routine includes the physical and mental routine that through repetition becomes habit.

> *Developing good Brain Management Skills during the Golf Shot Routine is the secret to increasing consistency and confidence.*

GOLF SHOT ROUTINE
- Assess and Analyze target and shot conditions
- Commit to Target and your Single Cue
- Walk into the shot, set up, keeping your cue
- Back off if distracted by internal or external distractions or extra thoughts or images
- Execute the shot
- Hold the follow-through and process a positive thought

GOLF MENTAL MANAGEMENT INTAKE
Please take the following intake to become aware of how you are managing your brain when practicing and playing golf. Completing this Intake will give you insight about *how you are managing your brain.*

First, select a specific shot on a course that you play often and answer these questions related to that shot.

List your most common thoughts during the phases of The Golf Shot Routine:

INTAKE:

1. As you approach the ball, your most common thoughts or images *before* club selection are:

_____

_____

_____

2. Once you have selected your club and are standing behind the ball, your most common thoughts or images before you walk into the shot are:

_____

_____

_____

_____

3. Your most common thoughts or images *while* walking into the shot are:

_____

_____

_____

_____

4. Your most common thoughts or images *over* the ball before the execution are:

_____

_____

_____

_____

5. Your most common thoughts or images *during* the swing are:

_____

_____

_____

_____

6. Your most common thoughts or images *after* the execution while you are in your follow-through position are:

_____

_____

_____

_____

Note the amount of time that each of these steps take:

#1 and #2 preparation steps can vary in time from 10 seconds to two minutes.

#3 walking to the shot is three to five seconds.

#4 standing over the ball is two to eight seconds.

#5 the shot execution is one and a half to two seconds.

#6 after the shot time is as long as the ball is in the air... or rolling on the grass.

Through the use of the skill training in this book, you can define the most efficient way to *manage your brain* for those very short periods of time. Then, if you practice and execute that brain management, you could find a whole new way to play and enjoy golf.

GOLF SHOT ROUTINE

1. PREPARE ZONE

For Full Swing:

Using the analytical (left) part of your brain, get a big picture view of your shot possibilities and begin to see your target and your general lie situation. Consider all the factors that can influence the shot and ball flight and your club selection—the wind, the distance you want to hit the shot, the ground angle where your ball is resting, and the grass conditions around the ball. Focus on your target and where you want the ball to land. Take the risks of the landing areas into consideration and select the smartest target for your skill level. Once you decide where you want the ball to land, that defines your *target line*. Then determine the distance to that target and select your club based on those variables. The most common error for amateurs in club selection is overestimating how far you hit the ball. If you make that error, you will be likely to tense up and try to hit the longest and most perfect shot that you have ever hit. As you have experienced, that often just doesn't work. Instead, generally select the club that will allow you to swing a little easier. Great shots are hit only a few times by each golfer when they play—even pros. So play the odds. Select a club that you think will give you the best result even if you don't hit that rare perfect shot!

For Chipping:
Consider all the factors that can influence the shot and your club selection—the wind, the ground angle where your ball is resting, and grass conditions around the ball. Focus on your target and where you want the ball to land. Then select the club and take rehearsal swings to determine the length of swing and energy you will use to create the distance you want. With your feet together, align your clubface on your chosen target line. When you separate your feet, usually in an open position, you are ready to hit the chip.

For Putting:
Always regard the speed of the putt first. Ask "Is it uphill or downhill?" Then ask: "Will it break to the left, right, or roll straight?" Once you have read the putt, your target is determined by the line on which you want to start the ball. Do rehearsal putting strokes to rehearse the compact length of your putting stroke and energy you will use to create the distance you want.

SPECIAL INSTRUCTION ON PUTTING
Modern Putting Stroke Tips
1. Keep the stroke short and compact.
2. The putting stroke is a hit and hold, with a compact stroke.
3. Always hold the follow-through position.
4. Use a Putting Arc™ to practice and improve your putting stroke.

---

2. COMMITMENTS – MAKE YOUR COMMITMENTS IN THE PREPARE ZONE

Once you have selected your club and are standing behind the ball, before you walk into the shot: commit to the target and commit to your single cue. The single cue is based on your individual brain processing preferences as guided in Chapter 1 of this book.

3. WALKING INTO THE SHOT

Walk with a quiet brain into the shot. You will have already made your commitment to your target and single cue so there is really no conversation that needs to be carried on for these few seconds.

If you have distracting thoughts, caused internally or externally, back off a few steps, organize your single cue, and go back into your shot.

4. OVER THE BALL BEFORE EXECUTION

With your feet closer together than your normal stance width, take your time to get your club face aligned to your target and set your body in your golf address position. When you have completed that, separate your feet to be parallel to the line of intended ball flight. (There will be options for alignment to create draw, fade, or low shots.) Separating and setting your feet is the last set-up item. Once settled, it is time to execute the shot. This is a quiet brain time. You have already committed to your target and cue, so there is no need for additional self conversation.

(You should practice this mental and physical process many times, both away from the course and on the driving range, so it becomes a habit that you can easily access on the course.)

If you have distracting thoughts, caused internally or externally, back off a few steps, organize your single cue and go back into your shot.

5. EXECUTION – DURING THE SWING

The swing takes 1½ to 2 seconds. Other than your single cue, any conversation that your brain has at this time will only be distracting and cause errors in the swing action. Stay focused on the single cue and stay quiet. The single cue is based on your individual brain processing preferences as explored in Chapter 1.

6.   FINISH POSITION – AFTER THE EXECUTION

Managing your brain AFTER the swing is vital. Fortunately, every shot you hit will give you feedback. The habits that you create in dealing with that feedback will strengthen or weaken your game, short and/or long term. You will receive one of three options of feedback—the shot was good, bad, or just OK. How your brain habitually manages this feedback, both on the range and on the course, will allow you to face good and bad times with more ease and success.

Brain research has proven that the repetition of thoughts will become habit. Negative or positive thoughts can now be evaluated by measuring the energy and frequency of that energy in the brain, the energy that flows to the body during those thoughts, and the energy that flows out of the body during those thoughts. Research has proven that negative and positive thoughts have a totally different effect on the body and energy, short and long term.

Most golfers say very little if they hit a good shot, but they tend to be quite vocal, sometimes externally and usually internally, when they hit a shot they don't like. They tend to say very negative things to themselves and this becomes a habit that has serious consequences on the golfer's game, both in the present and future.

In Chapter 3 and Chapter 8, more information and current research on how the brain works will give you understanding, tools, and motivation to enhance your Golf Brain Management skills to help you avoid negative thinking and reap the consequences of positive thinking.

DISTRACTION

In today's world, it is easy to be distracted. Multi-task thinking is prevalent. While it may or may not be a desirable trait for our lives, *distraction* is absolutely the death knell for golfers. *Focus* is a word you hear often in reference to golf and all sports. There are many ways to create focus and the opposite of focus is distraction.

During the Golf Shot Routine, there is a particular way you will want to manage your brain. Distraction can happen at any time during that process and you will want to practice strategies to avoid distraction and the interference that it brings to your game.

What is distraction? It is a brain-triggering occurrence coming from either internal or external causes that changes the current thought or focus in your brain.

Example 1: An External Distraction

> On the 18th hole during a round at The Masters in Tiger Woods' early professional years, he was set to hit his iron up the hill onto the green when a police siren went off on a street outside the Augusta GC course. In the middle of his backswing, because of his ability to focus, he was able to stop his swing and back off. Interestingly, when he again got ready to hit, the siren was still blaring, but then it was no longer a distraction. Once he knew the siren was going to be there, he stayed focused and successfully executed the shot.

> External distractions happen all the time to golfers: our playing partners start talking or moving around, the greens crew drives a cart into our space, a helicopter might take flight. If the distraction jars our focus, it is better to step back, take a couple of seconds to regain our cue commitment, and get right back into the shot. Trying to fight through the distraction while over the ball can take just as much time and usually results in a bad shot.

Example 2: An Internal Distraction

These are thoughts triggered internally by the golfer that have become a habit. They include golf swing thoughts, frustrating thoughts, thoughts about scoring or other outcomes, etc.

Most of my students admit that they have made it a habit of thinking three to 10 thoughts over the ball, and some even made lists of those thoughts. The multiple thought patterns have become habit. As they work with me on improving their *single focus* in the Golf Shot Routine, they are often distracted by those old thoughts popping into their heads because they have become a habit. As you begin to identify your favorite cues and practice using single cues over your shots, your habits of thinking on the course will begin to change and you will create a new habit of staying in focus with a single thought.

No matter what those thoughts or images are, if you have more than one as you are over the shot, they will be a distraction.

Example 3: Another Internal Distraction

Random internal thoughts can also be internal distractions. Even though we may be focused, as we approach or get over the ball, a thought can pop into our mind. We often say to ourselves "Where did that come from?" As a young golfer, I would often get an image of having left the iron on and seeing it on the ironing board at home. The image would just come out of the blue, and I didn't understand it. But now I have learned that after a few times of having that image or thought, that image became a habit and showed up when I was under pressure. Because that is the way our brain works—repeated thoughts and images become a habit.

The other types of internal distractions are random thoughts that are based in two categories: 1) Thoughts about things happening in our life off the course—phone calls, business deals, and personal issues; 2) Thoughts based in our emotional past—what others might think about our shot, thinking about the final score, the positive or negative consequences of the shot we just hit, or even thinking of the consequences of playing well or playing poorly. There are strategies to change those thoughts and the more you practice those strategies, they will become a habit. Exercises in Chapter 3 and tools in Chapter 8 will explain those strategies and guide you away from distraction as you play.

What are your most common distractions while playing golf?

External Distractions that have happened to you once or repetitively?

1.
2.
3.
4.

Internal Distractions that have happened to you once or repetitively?

1.
2.
3.
4.

These thoughts can or may have become bad habits. They can be imbedded in your memory. But you can change that memory bank. There will be more in Chapter 3 and Chapter 8 on that.

The Starting Point for staying focused and ridding the distractions while playing golf is the following: *Commit to a single cue and be aware of distractions.*

When those distractions appear in your brain, back off the shot, and start over with the single focused cue you had committed to. If you don't back off, your brain just thinks you are fine with those distracting thoughts and will continue to keep them as a habit. When you do back off, you are breaking the habit of that distraction and beginning a new good habit. After a few practice sessions on the range and on the course, you will begin to build the habit of *focus* on a singular cue and the distracting thoughts will be less likely to enter.

IMPORTANT!

In high pressure situations, a negative or random thought may flash back and bring old distractions up again, but if you have trained yourself to back off when you are aware of their presence, you can get refocused to the present.

Staying in the present is vital. If you are still thinking about a shot or hole in the past or contemplating your future score or other future outcomes, you are not in the present. None of those past or future thoughts will bring a focused "in the present" experience or cue. So, in fact, thoughts in the past or in the future during your Golf Shot Routine are a distraction.

CHAPTER 3

HABITS PRODUCE CONSISTENCY

HOW to Create New Habits

Neuroscientific research has proven the following:

Forming a new habit requires single focus repetition. Repetition daily for 20 to 30 days of a single focus, whether it is physical or mental, will create a habit. It takes more days of repetition to embed that habit strongly enough to repeat it under pressure.

In medical terms, this repetition is defined as myelination. The memory of a physical motion has been mis-identified through the years as "muscle memory." While the body's cells have DNA that has some memory capacity, the memory itself is made in the brain. When a physical action or a thought occurs, neurons connect via axons and dendrites at a synapse connection. The brain has a process of encapsulating the connected axons in a white matter defined as myelin. The repetition of a physical motion or thought over an axon is reinforced by the myelination of that chain of axon/neuron connections. And that is why you can tie your shoes with no thought and perform many activities that have become habit. Those actions have been myelinated.

The main purpose of a myelin layer (or sheath) is to increase the speed at which impulses propagate along the myelinated fiber. Once an action or thought is myelinated, it will occur more easily and quickly.

The old saying "Perfect practice makes perfect" is so true. What you repeat will myelinate. If you want to learn the golf swing or other golf skills, repeat single-focused segments of those skills for 20 to 30 days and they will be a habit.

Excellent resources to explore myelination further are the book *The Talent Code* by Daniel Cole and the article "White Matter" by R. Douglas Fields in the March 1, 2008 issue of *Scientific American*.

When working on improving your golf game, you will want to form the best habits you can in the following areas to create Consistency and Confidence:

1. **Physical Skill Training for all aspects of the game—full swing, chipping, and putting**

2. **Golf Shot Routine—four phases**

Physical Skill Training

Limit the repetitions for skill training to one item at a time with repetitions in sets of 15 to 20 minutes. The brain can focus on repeating 1 item at a time and that will become a habit. In the example on the Physical Skill Training Schedule Chart, the golfer chose to first practice (A) Balanced Finish with sets of 15 to 20 minutes in repetitions, and then (B) The Take Away with 15 to 20 minutes of repetitions. Depending upon the individual and the difficulty of the physical skill that is being learned, within 20 to 30 days, the habit of A and B will be formed and will begin to become part of the natural golf swing. Double the days of repetition and the habit will be more likely to hold up under pressure.

Physical Skill Training repetitions are best done away from hitting balls, either at home or at the range but not hitting balls. When the ball is introduced during Habit Repetitions, your brain changes its focus from the physical skill training to hitting the shot and having expectations of the shot results. Practicing physical skill training while hitting balls will only delay the habit-forming process.

My students have had great success doing their Physical Skill repetitions without hitting balls. Information about how to best integrate the Physical Skill Training with the Golf Shot Routine is covered later in this chapter.

PHYSICAL SKILL TRAINING SCHEDULE

Sample Physical Skill	Number of Days	Time of Repetitions per Session	Dates of Repetition
Balanced Finish	20 to 30	15 to 20 min.	30 boxes to check complete
Take Away	20 to 30	15 to 20 min.	30 boxes to check complete

PHYSICAL SKILL TRAINING SCHEDULE

Physical Skill	Number of Days	Time of Repetitions per Session	Dates of Repetition
_____	_____	_____	_____
_____	_____	_____	_____
_____	_____	_____	_____
_____	_____	_____	_____
_____	_____	_____	_____
_____	_____	_____	_____
_____	_____	_____	_____
_____	_____	_____	_____
_____	_____	_____	_____
_____	_____	_____	_____

Use the above chart to schedule any Physical Skill Training that you want to do.

Golf Shot Routine Training

This is an excellent mental golf training system you can use to become Consistent and Confident.

This practice can be done on the range, short game practice area, and on the course. Practice executing each shot with your new Golf Shot Routine (described in Chapter 2) during practice sessions and then in practice rounds on the course until it becomes a habit. Again, 20 - 30 days will begin the process and more practice will make it easier to repeat under pressure.

Golf Shot Routine Zones	Action during Segment
1. PREPARE ZONE	Assess: Wind Lie Target Conditions Select Target Select Club Commit to Target Commit to Single Cue
2 WALKING INTO SHOT	Practice Quiet Mind
3. OVER THE BALL	Align the clubface, Set Up and Get comfortable Focus on Single Cue Back off if there is a Distraction
4. EXECUTE SHOT	Single Cue or Quiet Mind
5. FINISH SHOT	Hold finish, observe shot, Express Positive Feedback

Integrating the Physical Skill Training with Golf Shot Routine Training
Repeat the Physical Skill that you are training away from the golf ball before adding hitting the ball to the training. When you first begin to hit balls, you will want to focus on that physical change as the single cue for each swing.

Using Single Cues to Create and Change Physical Swing Skills

Important Reminder: *Use Only One Cue Per Shot!!* After you have practiced single physical swing changes away from the ball for the 20-30 days, they will begin to become habit. When you are ready to hit balls during a physical swing change, select a single physical swing cue and hit a series of five to 10 balls with that single cue. Repetition of the single physical swing cue as you begin to hit balls will assist in making that physical skill a habit. After a period of time, that move will be habit and not require any thought direction. A single physical swing cue that matches your sensory system and brain preference will not be a distraction, but using more than one cue will distract the brain and interfere with a natural swing. As you adopt this system, you will be tempted to use more than one cue—unfortunately most golfers are trying to use numerous cues as they execute. Those multiple cues are major distractions to the brain's ability to deliver the golf swing to the body. Not all shots will be perfect, but using single focus cues will improve the consistency.

Using Single Cues to Create "In the Zone" Experiences

Important Reminder: *One Cue Per Shot!!*

Chapter 1 guided you to begin the discovery of your *favorite cues*, based on your learning preferences. When you go to the range before the round, hit some balls and let your imagination lead you to the cue for the day. If a magic cue does not occur, select one of your cues from your *favorite cues* to use for the day.

The purpose of each part of the Golf Shot Routine is to manage your thoughts and allow you to more often release your natural physical golf swing for best results. Practice this routine often on the range to create the habit for the course.

The Positive Statement on the Finish is an extremely important part of this process. No matter what the results of the shot are, you must make a Positive Statement, either silently or out loud. Golf is a hard game and a normal golfer will only hit three or four really good shots per round. Other shots will be OK or not what we want. Therefore, most golfers are saying negative things often after many shots. The problem is that the habit that is being developed with those negative thoughts creates an environment in which negative thoughts can become prevalent throughout the entire shot process. In that process, we lose the expectation of hitting a good shot. Instead, the brain is so used to saying something critical or negative that we are actually making that a habit in our shot processing.

If the shot you hit is not exactly what you wanted, use one of the following Positive Statements.

- Good Shot
- That's OK
- Good contact
- Good direction

Or, under the worst circumstances: Nice day today...

After you have made your Positive Statement in your Finish, and you have completed holding your balanced finish, you can reflect on anything you like about the shot or its outcome. The mind is generally a problem solver and will naturally want to analyze a bit or a lot.

WARNING: Do not take the thoughts of the bad shot or the imagined remedy of the bad shot to the next shot. **Every new shot has to be done with the Golf Shot Routine which does not allow you to think about your last shot as you execute in the present. Stay in the present with each and every shot and use the Golf Shot Routine to help manage your brain to keep it in the present.** With every new shot, focus on *creating* a good shot, not trying to fix a prior bad one. As you approach each shot, you need to use your Golf Shot Routine and there is no room for negative thoughts or swing fixing thoughts in that Routine.

Playing golf with the Golf Shot Routine allows you to manage your brain in every shot and focus on execution, rather than being in the past or the future. The Golf Shot Routine will keep you in the present with the shot you are currently hitting.

CHAPTER 4

GOLF EQUIPMENT

The History of Club Fitting

In the 1700s, as golf was growing in Scotland, golfers spent countless days in their back sheds, winding hickory shafts to iron pieces and wooden heads with leather straps, and adding leather wrapped grips at the top end.

We've come a long way, baby. Today, structural engineers sit at sophisticated computers designing and redesigning heads and shafts, based on advanced laws of physics to make the hit feel sweeter and more consistent and sending the ball a long way. They've substituted the wood, leather, and iron for graphite, steel, titanium, composite grips and heads, and even hi-tech hosel and head adjustments.

And yes, the ball goes farther, the hit is sweeter and more forgiving, and the combination of components that can make up the club is astounding.

So what is missing? There is still a major missing piece despite the enormous progress of the golf equipment industry.

While all the sophisticated engineering has improved the component parts, 80% of golf equipment used by amateur golfers is not serving them well, not helping them improve their swing, shots, or their enjoyment of the game. Even many golf professionals don't have golf equipment that is enhancing their athletic ability to make consistent shots. But because the golf professionals are incredible athletes, their ability to compensate or adapt to poorly-fitted equipment is easier than for most amateurs.

As controversial as this might be, the truth is that the golf industry could be doing a much better job in delivering golf equipment that is good for the golf consumer.

Think about it: Golfers come in all sizes and physical strengths—from juniors under four feet tall to golfers as tall as seven feet. The physical strength can be observed in golfers who generate a club head speed that will hit a drive less than 100 yards to a club head speed that drives the ball almost 400 yards.

Proper Club Fitting is the only way that golfers can reliably discover and own golf clubs that will suit their bodies, their physical strengths and weaknesses, their range of motion, their learning modes, and thereby enhance their game.

This chapter tells the truth about Club Fitting. The facts are controversial, but it's a story that needs to be told. As you begin to learn the history of club fitting, I hope that you will become an informed consumer and find a way to get clubs that are really fitted properly for you.

The Timeline

1972

Karsten Solheim, founder of PING, designed a plan to custom fit clubs to the individual golfer. He based PING fitting on measuring a player's height and fingertip-to-ground distance as well as the grip size of each player.

1983

The Henry-Griffitts Golf Club Company began the first Dynamic Club Fitting process—fitting the golf club to the individual while watching each golfer hit balls. Gary Blaisdell led their training programs and charted new territory for Henry-Griffitts worldwide.

1992

Slazenger Golf USA launched the most comprehensive and sophisticated Club Fitting System to come to the market. As Vice President of Slazenger Golf, Gary Blaisdell spearheaded the Slazenger program and that led to many other golf club companies entering the custom club fitting business in the mid to late 1990s. Those companies included Titleist, Taylor Made, Callaway, Cobra, Mizuno, NIKE, and several smaller start-ups.

Thus, the Club Fitting era was born.

However, there were a few major problems that affected the success of this market approach:

1. Inadequate training of the club fitters.

2. Inadequate support for the club fitters at their home club, once they had received minimal training from the manufacturer.

3. The decreased profit margins for the manufacturer due to the cost of supporting the fitters and fitting training and building of the custom sets.

4. For customers who did have experienced and qualified fitters, the average time they kept their clubs before purchasing a new set was nearly 11 years. This was especially problematic for manufacturers intent on selling golfers new clubs or sets as often as possible.

1999

The Slazenger program was discontinued under new corporate brand ownership, and ever since then the industry has continued to "dumb down" the process, in a deliberate attempt to remove the golf professional from the fitting equation, and hire their own team of "experts" to do "demo days." The professional-centered club fitting experience is essentially dead.

Due to these factors, the consumer, initially gung-ho to get fitted and buy a new set, began to have bad experiences in buying fitted clubs that did not improve their game because they really were not properly fitted.

Disillusionment set in for the consumer and they began to dismiss club fitting as a valid service.

The manufacturers wanted to sell more equipment, so many of them de-emphasized their club fitting programs and relied more heavily on the traditional marketing and sales strategies of TV and Tour Professional endorsements.

Today
PING, Henry-Griffitts, and Mizuno are still promoting the importance of club fitting. Even for them, however, the task of training and getting industry support for well-trained club fitters is problematic. Small club fitting stores and a few major manufacturer fitting centers have opened in major golf markets, but the training of their club fitters, the engineering expertise, and support from the manufacturers makes their results unpredictable.

Through the years, I have relied heavily on Gary Blaisdell, a truly exceptional club fitting expert. I want to tell you about Gary. He was head golf professional at The Tucson National Resort and Spa where I was putting on an LPGA regional championship when we first met in 1982. In 1989, Gary joined the newly formed Henry-Griffitts Company and became their Education Director and Vice President of Sales. For four years, Gary trained professionals throughout the world to fit and sell Henry-Griffitts golf clubs and helped them solidify their fitting concepts and sales and marketing processes.

Unfortunately, of the hundreds of club fitters that Gary trained, fewer than 10% still have any activity in club fitting.

In 1993, Gary founded Slazenger Custom Clubs as a division of the Slazenger Golf Club Company and again trained hundreds of golf professionals at the best private and resort clubs in the U.S. and Canada. During all those years, we worked together to assure that fitting and teaching were well integrated.

In 1999, the Maxfli Dunlop Company went through bankruptcy in England and the brands were sold to Taylor Made by the bankruptcy court. Slazenger was owned by Maxfli Dunlop and following the sale, the Slazenger custom club division was closed. Gary moved back to Arizona and formed his own company, Blaisdell Performance Systems, Inc. Since then, he has fitted and sold thousands of sets of clubs using primarily PING, Mizuno, Taylor Made, Callaway, and some NIKE products. We continue to work on the integration of club fitting and teaching, striving to provide excellence for all clients.

By working with Gary, I learned what follows in this chapter on Club Fitting advice. His contact information is available on the PMG Website www.powermentalgolf.com. I highly recommend that you call, email, and visit him in Arizona to experience excellence in club fitting.

Logical Truth

With many purchases in life, one size does fit all—but not in golf equipment. When you purchase golf clubs, you usually have the following choices: Junior, Women, Senior, and Men. Within the Women and Senior categories you have the choice of one shaft strength and length. In the Men's category, the choices might be two lengths and generally two shaft strengths. In the Junior category, the industry has expanded the options to three lengths to adapt for a youngster's growth.

The last time I was people watching at the airport or on my lesson tee, I noticed that people come in many more varieties of size and strength than that.

Some women are very tall, but not strong enough to handle the shaft strength or weight of a men's club. Women's clubs were designed, typically, for a 5' to 5'4" woman. What about all the women who are 5'5" and taller? What about all the women who are taller than 5'10"?

Some men are tall. The golf club was designed for a 5'6" to 5'10" man. What about all the men who are 5'11" and taller? What about the 6'4" to 6'11" man?

Of course the strength of people within all the categories vary tremendously. That is why club fitting was started—to adapt to the individual's size and physical strength.

I enjoy snow skiing. When you buy or rent snow skis, there is a well-trained process to fit skis to the individual's body weight, strength, and experience. The buyer signs a liability release that says they were fitted. Even though most golfers don't fall down and break bones with a poorly fitted golf club, it's too bad that the brain damage due to the disappointing shots doesn't create a liability issue as fitting snow skis does.

If a club is properly fitted for the individual golfer, when the golfer makes a good swing they are often rewarded with a good shot. When they make an off-balance swing, they are rewarded with an errant shot. But when a golfer has equipment that is *not* the right fit for them, when they make a good swing, they may get an errant shot and begin to make corrections, compensations, and create bad swing habits to make that club give them the shot they want.

Many students say, "It's not the club; it's me." But once they have a properly fitted club in their hands and hit rewarding shots, they say "You were right—it *was* the club, not me." It is always the question: the Indian or the Arrow? Granted, properly fitted clubs will not create great shots all the time or eliminate some of our errant shots, but the odds of more successful performance goes up dramatically with properly fitted equipment.

Why Properly Fitted Clubs are Important

The most important key to a consistent golf swing is a balanced set-up and balanced finish. If your clubs are too short, your balance at set-up will not be properly or athletically centered. And as the swing is executed, balance is more difficult to maintain for players who have clubs that are too long or short for them. For examples, look at the following tour players' set up positions with their short and mid-irons:

Group 1 (TALL)

Dustin Johnson, Matt Kuchar, Bradley Keegan, and Bubba Watson.

Compare their set up positions with average height players who have a better club length for their body style.

Group 2 (AVERAGE)

Jordan Spieth, Rory McIlroy, Jason Day, Zach Johnson, Billy Hoershel.

In the first group (TALL), their irons are too short for their body design and in the second group (AVERAGE), their irons are better length for their body design. If the clubs are too short for the individual player, they will not be able to keep their balance during the swing, and have to stand taller during the backswing and then move back down to the shot to make impact. They have to measure the up and down motion in addition to the regular turning motion of the swing. Charles Barkley's swing is an example of this. Barkley's up and down movement in his downswing was documented on the *Golf Channel Instruction* show. That downswing move was his creative way to measure back down to the ball with golf clubs that were many inches too short for him.

These professional golfers are all elite athletes and in Group 1, each of the players compensates in a different way during their swing to keep good balance and then finish in balance. The players in Group 2 do not have the challenge of compensating for clubs that are too short for them. If most amateurs, not being elite athletes, have clubs that are the improper length, they will have more difficulty creating the compensations that the golf professionals can create.

There are at least 29 elements that can be adjusted in building any golf club. Of course, the ideal circumstance would be to have all clubs in the set have all elements the same. Having every club feel the same during the swing allows the golfer to swing without adapting or compensating for a club that is built differently.

An Exercise to Evaluate your Golf Clubs

What are your favorite clubs in your set? _____

Do you have a club or clubs in your set that you don't like to use because they are so unpredictable? If yes, which clubs? _____

Have you considered that the clubs you don't like may have been built differently? (It is not unusual for a manufacturer to include clubs in the same set that are not built with like elements. In proper club fitting, clubs in your set can be measured and compared. This often exposes the mismatched clubs in the set.)

If you have a club that is not matched you will not be able to get consistent results.

Do you identify with any of the above? _____

The 10 Club Fitting Issues that Can Change Your Game

1. Shaft Length

"It's not just how tall you are, it is HOW you are tall."

Let's call this the "Tall X Factor" for club fitting. When you take an excellent golf set-up position, the important factor is to have the club long enough to allow a tall, well balanced set-up as shown in all the set-up graphics below. That set-up has the knees barely bent and a forward tip from the hips with straight back. The set-up should not have deeply bent knees or an excessive tilt at the hips.

While everyone should learn about club fitting and get clubs that are best fit for them, there are particular groups of golfers who have a higher probability that standard clubs will not be long enough for them.

The "Tall X Factor" should be measured with a 6 or 7 iron.

Graphics 1 and 4 below depict a man and woman golfer, each of AVERAGE height and build.

Graphics 2, 3, 5, and 6 portray men and women who are taller than average with equally proportioned legs and torso.

Graphics 7, 8, 9, 10, 11, and 12 portray men and women with longer legs and shorter torsos. They fit into the group that will need longer irons.

If you are barrel chested or have a broader core or tummy, you are a likely candidate for longer clubs, as illustrated in Graphics 13 and 14.

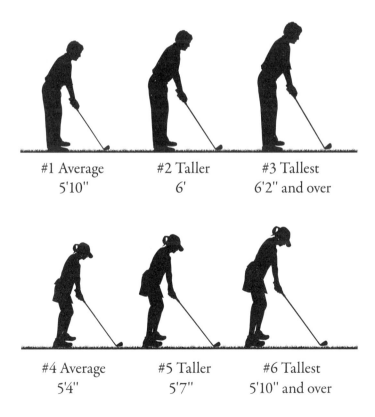

| #1 Average | #2 Taller | #3 Tallest |
| 5'10" | 6' | 6'2" and over |

| #4 Average | #5 Taller | #6 Tallest |
| 5'4" | 5'7" | 5'10" and over |

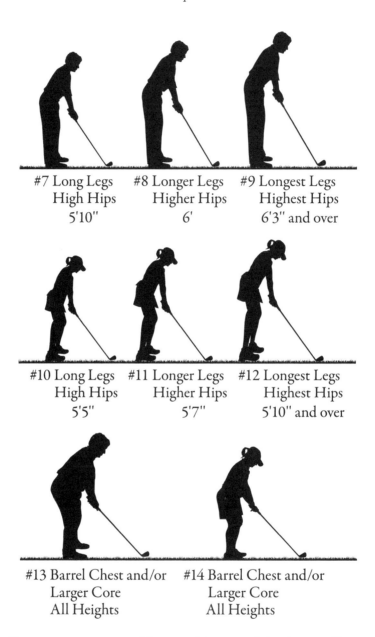

#7 Long Legs   #8 Longer Legs   #9 Longest Legs
High Hips   Higher Hips   Highest Hips
5'10"   6'   6'3" and over

#10 Long Legs   #11 Longer Legs   #12 Longest Legs
High Hips   Higher Hips   Highest Hips
5'5"   5'7"   5'10" and over

#13 Barrel Chest and/or   #14 Barrel Chest and/or
Larger Core   Larger Core
All Heights   All Heights

The taller or more stout golfers need longer clubs (especially irons) in order for the golfer to be able to create the set-up with a tall, well-balanced position allowing and promoting them to swing with balance, staying tall, without moving up and down during the swing.

If you determine that you need longer clubs, the challenge for you will be *where* you can find longer clubs, and to get the right shaft and overall weight. Most of the current manufacturers offer only up to 1 1/2 inches over regular length in their club fitting centers. If you buy clubs off the rack that are not special ordered, the standard length is usually only what is available.

I have worked with many golfers, men, women, and juniors who need over 1½ inches longer. Clubs with longer lengths cannot be purchased from most golf courses, stores, or from the traditional manufacturers. Blaisdell Performance Systems can have clubs built up to 4 inches over length, while keeping the weights in a manageable range. As the club is built longer it generally becomes heavier to swing. Just as the length is important, it is also important that the club be light enough to swing with comfort, balance, and maximum club head speed. While most manufacturers do not build long and light clubs, Blaisdell Performance Systems worked with major manufacturers to create engineering processes that accomplish the long but lighter club. Gary Blaisdell can fit you and order those longer, lighter clubs.

Attention: Tall Women and Tall Men

Do not spend your hard-earned dollars on golf clubs designed for the "average height" golfer. Your golf clubs should allow you to set up in good athletic posture and good balance, just as any shorter person can and as the graphics indicate.

2. Grip size

Being sure that the size of your grip fits your hands is very important. Grips are now made in many sizes and it is easy to get a grip size that will enhance your hand connection to the club. If the grip is too small or too big, the grip may move during the swing and/or your fingernails could make improper contact with the palm of your hand. Proper grip size is very important and needs to fit both the size of your palm and length of your fingers.

3. Shaft flex

Shaft flexes have been traditionally labeled as L (Ladies), (SR) Senior, (R) Regular, S (Stiff) and X (Extra Stiff). For the last 25 years, it has been possible to measure shaft strength by cycles—which measures the stiffness of a shaft in the number of cycles per minute that shaft will vibrate when set in motion. Within each of the categories—L, SR, R, S, and X—there are a number of different cycle categories. If you are a professional or very low handicap player, you might want to have your shafts exactly matched by cycles.

A big problem with buying clubs that are not custom fit and built is that shafts within sets coming from the factories have often not been measured and matched within the set. For years we have measured our client's clubs and 70% of the time, if the clubs were not custom fit, the shafts within the set did not match. When they don't match, the shots from the unmatched clubs are usually noticeably not as good for your success. If you have a club or two or more in your set that just do not feel like the others and create bad shots too often, it's likely the shafts are not matching.

4. Loft Degree on the Driver

There is a misunderstanding about Driver Loft. The myth is that the lower the loft the further the ball goes. That is just not the case. Driver lofts vary from 7.5 to 15 degrees. You should buy the loft that matches your club head speed. Most people don't know their club head speed. So let's talk instead about how far you hit your driver, because club head speed is one of the main contributing factors to distance. The squareness of the hit in the face is the other most important contributing factor to distance.

The list below is a starting point as you test drivers.

Driver Distance	Driver Loft
100 yards	15 degrees
150	14
175	12
200	11
225	10.5
250	10
275	9.5
300	9.0 - 9.5
300+	8.0 – 9.5

Matching the correct shaft flex and flex point with the loft is vital to creating the maximum distance possible.

Follow this thinking for a minute. If you have a driver that does not have enough loft and you hit a few balls low, you will hang back on your right side to get underneath the ball to get it in the air. That will cause you to lose your power and eventually cause bad swing compensations.

The reason a player with a higher swing speed and therefore more distance can use a driver with less loft is because the speed of their swing creates more flex in the shaft. As the club head explodes into the ball, the shaft releases and puts more loft on the club head. At a slower club head speed, you need to have more loft built into the club head. That is also why it is easier for most golfers to hit their 3 wood and other fairway woods off the tee because they have more loft than the driver and are generally easier to hit squarely and get airborne than a driver with an inappropriate amount of loft.

Don't automatically believe your golf buddy or a salesman who tells you that you will hit the ball farther with a lower degree of loft on your driver. Instead, match the driver loft to your distance and/or your club head speed. And do a demo test on the driver before you purchase.

5. Loft Degree on Fairway Woods

Players with high club head speed can easily handle hitting a 3 wood off the ground. If the golfer's club head speed is lower than the pros or excellent amateurs, the fairway wood selection should be more lofted: 4 or 5 wood and, for the slower club head speeds, even 7 and 9 woods may be the best fairway woods. Again, experiment with different fairway wood lofts to find the best loft and launch for you. The concept is the same: Higher club head speeds loft the ball more easily. Slower club head speeds loft the ball at a much lower trajectory.

Here's an example. If you are inconsistent with a 3 wood off the ground, make your 4 or 5 wood your "go-to" fairway club. You will get better loft and more consistent hits. Even though you might think the 3 wood would go longer, hitting a lot of errant 3 woods will not help you enjoy your game or improve your score. This loft concept is why Tour Professionals do not hit their driver off the fairway. They are talented enough to hit occasional great shots "off the deck" as they call hitting it off the grass with their driver, but with the lower driver loft they will be less consistent than they will be with their 3 wood.

6. Hybrids to replace long irons

For all levels of golfers, the hybrids (also called *rescue clubs*) have replaced the long irons in the golf bag. Their popularity in the last eight years has skyrocketed. For professionals and good amateur players with mid-to-higher club head speeds, the hybrid can replace the 2, 3, and 4 irons. For the player with slower club head speed, the hybrid can replace the 4, 5, and 6 irons.

The hybrids are easier to hit than the long irons due to the design of the small hybrid head. It has more of the design of a fairway wood, has better weight balance in the head than an iron, and has a wider sweet spot that creates "better misses" and is usually lighter in weight than the long irons. Making a switch from the long irons to hybrids can take strokes off your game right away. It is an excellent golf equipment investment. There are no standard industry specifications for the lofts or numbers on the hybrids. When buying a hybrid club, be sure the shaft matches your irons and other woods and experiment with different brands of hybrids to find the loft, look, and feel you like. Generally speaking, higher lofts relate to a more forgiving club. Again, test them before you buy.

7. Weight of the Club

The swing weight of the club is just that: the weight of the club as it is being swung. The traditional weighting system for golf clubs is defined by letter and number.

The swing weight is defined like this:

Lightest swing weight is in the "C" ranges from C1 to C9.
The heavier swing weights are in the "D" ranges from D0 to D9.

Most men's clubs fall in the C9 to D3 range of swing weights and most women's and seniors' clubs weigh in the C3 to C8 range. Clubs have gotten lighter in the last 10 years, especially the driver, hybrids, and woods.

Many golfers are very sensitive to the weight of the club, either on the light or heavy side. Golfers with a slower club head speed will tend to create consistent club head speed and endurance throughout the round with lighter swing weight in their clubs. Be careful when purchasing to buy a club that is light enough for you to swing with maximum club head speed. If you are a strong lower handicap golfer you may like the feel of the little heavier swing weight. Whenever possible, hit clubs before you purchase to get a feel for the weight and look of the club head and to see the ball flight the club creates.

8. Lie Angle of the Irons

The lie angle of the irons is important for consistent direction. In simplest terms, the lie angle is the attitude at which the club head impacts the ground from heel to toe through the bottom of the swing arc. Ideally, you would want the bottom of the club to be flat to the ground during impact.

If the club is too upright for your natural swing, at impact the toe will be up and the club will not be flat to the ground. The directional influence of this error would cause the ball to go to the left of the target for a right-handed player and to the right for a left-handed player. The more lofted clubs, 8 iron through wedge, will have greater off line error than the less lofted 7, 6, 5, 4, and 3 irons. The lie angle must be neutralized so as not to influence the directional flight of the ball whatsoever.

If your short irons tend to move off line more than your other clubs, I recommend that you have your loft/lie angles checked. If you find that your lie angle is too upright or too flat, your brain has been working overtime to use one swing for the short irons and a different swing for the mid and long irons. With all that compensation, you may not be sure which swing to use for your driver and woods.

One of the greatest causes of inconsistency and loss of confidence is the lack of organization that occurs if your golf clubs are not properly fit.

9. Specific to Women

Be sure that your clubs are light. If you are over 5'4" or if you have high hips, you are probably a candidate for longer clubs, but be sure they are light. If your fingers are long and you wear your nails longer, you will want to be fit for larger grips. The proper shaft flex will be important to create maximum distance and accurate direction. If you have a choice, it is better to go with a more flexible shaft. If you hit your driver less than 160 yards, Ladies' Flex is right for you. If you hit your driver 160 to 210 yards, Senior Shaft will be good for you. If you hit your driver over 210, you should test a Men's Regular Shaft.

10. Specific to Juniors

The length and weight of your clubs and shaft flex are the MOST important factors to consider. Also, grip size is critical. There is a wide variety of small and junior grips available. The lighter the club and more flexible the shaft, the easier the game will be to learn and have fun. Juniors should especially avoid heavy clubs with stiff shafts.

So What Can You Do?

On the Power Mental Golf website www.powermentalgolf.com there is an assessment tool and more information to get you started. Gary Blaisdell is in Arizona and is available for fittings and lessons as well. He is known throughout the industry as one of the finest club fitters and instructors in the country.

A closing thought: Buyer Beware! Believe your own sense and feel when buying new clubs. I recommend that you always try to hit the clubs you are considering buying before your purchase. Many retail golf and sports stores, some public driving ranges, and some private clubs allow you to hit demonstration clubs on the range or in the store.

CHAPTER 5

NEW COMPUTER TECHNOLOGY: MENTAL AND MEDICAL

Mental Game Technology is about validating your ability to manage your brain. I often ask my students, "Who is managing your brain today?"

I have always taught my students that the mental aspect of the game of golf is the most important thing for success in the game. I have used books, seminars, tapes, CDs, personal mentors—anything I can find—to help guide my golf students to better "manage their brain."

We are living in interesting and exciting times… times where cutting-edge technology and innovative science have brought us to a point where a computer can guide you to *better manage your brain.*

New computer technology, using information from many years of brain research, is going to make playing golf easier and more fun. It is also giving players increased confidence and consistency. This new computer technology guides you to manage your brain and trains you to get "Into the Zone."

In all the history of golf, I think that this is the most significant positive change to golf instruction, playing better golf, and increasing the enjoyment of the game.

The best way to begin to learn to manage your brain is to follow the system recommended in the first seven chapters of this book:

1. Identify your individual learning and processing preferences and use that knowledge to explore your connection to the target, your ability to stay focused, to be relaxed and get "In the Zone."

2. Use daily repetition of new golf skills that you want to learn, away from the ball and then with single focus while hitting balls until they become a habit.

3. Have an expert club fitting to be sure your clubs are properly fit for you.

4. Design a Golf Shot Routine that is fit to your learning and processing preferences and make it a habit. Get "Into the Zone."

5. Armed with that information and preparation, the new computer technology discussed in this chapter will validate when you successfully create the desired state of mind and get "Into the Zone." With practice, you will become increasingly aware of the state of your brain and use that awareness in practice and on the course to play with increased confidence and consistency.

I began using this revolutionary technology in November of 2015. Since then, I have used it with my students and every student has had remarkable results, both in becoming more aware of their mental state and validating the strategies they had learned to create the "In the Zone" experience. With this validation, their golf games have improved and they all have reported that their ability to find calmness and single focus has greatly improved.

The research behind the new technology
Research has revealed that there is a defined state of brain frequencies that occur when the athlete is having "In the Zone" experiences. The brain is constantly emitting frequencies and with electroencephalograph (EEG) technology, brain frequencies can be measured. Research has also proven

that through feedback, the human being can control, change, and manage their brain frequencies. Nueroscience research has now proved that when an athlete successfully manages brain frequencies during performance, performance improves. With management of their brain frequencies, the athlete can stay in a comfortable state and create "The Zone." "The Zone" is defined as the state of being very relaxed, in the present, and focused. That makes success in athletic performance easier to attain. Most people can identify when they are "In the Zone," but don't know **how** to get **"Into** the Zone." The new technology trains a player to move "Into the Zone" and validates when they have accomplished the shift.

At least four portable products are currently in the market. All are based on brain frequency research. The new technology is portable electroencephalograph (EEG) machines that monitor neural activity in the brain. Using these portable EEG machines to train the management of brain frequencies will allow an athlete to get "Into the Zone" and know when they are there.

The portable EEG products in the market are: FocusBand, MUSE™, Emotiv, and Versus. They are portable EEG machines that have been tested by medical professionals and in training with athletes. FocusBand and MUSE™ are the two technologies that have been tested with golfers. Both FocusBand and MUSE™ are wearable headbands that measure the brain frequencies and give immediate feedback through apps on the smart phone or IPad®.

FocusBand

FocusBand has been tested for two years with PGA Tour Players. Jason Day was the first player to make a significant performance improvement using FocusBand. Jason began playing professional golf in Australia in 2004 and has been on the U.S. PGA Tour since 2006. By 2011, he was a winner of two PGA Tour tournaments and in 2012 was ranked 37th in the World Golf Rankings. He was however, having trouble closing out the win especially in Major Tournaments.

He began using the FocusBand in 2013, coached by Jason Goldsmith, a performance coach, and Henry Boulton, who, with his father Graham, invented the FocusBand. After he began working with the FocusBand technology in 2013, Day improved enough to reach 11th in the world rankings and then reached 8th in 2014. In 2015, using the FocusBand, he won four PGA Tour events and his first Major, the 2015 PGA Championship and, in May 2016, The Player's Championship. In September of 2015, he became #1 in the world rankings and recaptured that ranking in 2016. He credits the FocusBand with contributing to that success.

Designed to be the most efficient and customer friendly portable EEG in the golf and sports industry, FocusBand enables you to measure & train the process to change the result, increasing mindfulness and staying in the present.

The FocusBand is a wearable, portable EEG device with three sensors that are built into the headband that measure brain activity. The neoprene headset and the woven sensors are perspiration tolerant and the measured data is displayed on an app downloaded to a Smartphone or IPad® and connects via Bluetooth. Music tones are used to assist in the neurofeedback training to self regulate emotional levels and to get "Into The Zone." In sports training, the FocusBand is currently being used in baseball, basketball, cricket, tennis, volleyball, soccer, and golf.

PGA Tour players who have been training with the FocusBand include Jason Day, Justin Rose, Padraig Harrington, Rod Pampling, Greg Chalmers, Mike Weir, D.J. Trahan, Daniel Summerhays, and Chris Stroud.

To learn more about the FocusBand, visit The Power of Mental Golf *website:* *www.powermentalgolf.com*

MUSE™ with Software OptiBrain and OptiTrain

In 2015, Dr. Debbie Crews, led Opti International™ to design a golf-focused software app for the MUSE™ headband that can be downloaded to a mobile device. The MUSE™ with the Opti software allows the user to monitor their neural activity in real time via a mobile device. It can be used to improve golf focus and is also a useful tool for researchers and app developers who want to start capturing and tracking brainwave data.

MUSE™, a lightweight portable EEG (electroencephalography) machine, is housed in a headband that lets users monitor their neural activity in real time and helps them meditate, manage stress and boost concentration. It was originally designed to be used by therapists and doctors to enable clients to manage stress and boost their mood, facilitate living well with anxiety, pain, and depression.

Opti International™, after designing the OptiBrain and OptiTrain software, added a stretch headband that fits over the hard case headband that allows movement for the golfer while training.

The women's golf teams at Arizona State University and the University of Virginia are training with the Opti Software. Professional ice skaters and baseball pitchers have also trained with the MUSE™ headbands.

To learn more about MUSE™ and Opti Software, visit The Power of Mental Golf *website:* *www.powermentalgolf.com*

What Can a Portable EEG Device Do for You?
The FocusBand and MUSE™ with Opti software validate for the user how their brain frequency is measuring in real time.

The important progress of these technologies is that for the first time a golfer can identify when they are "In the Zone." Practicing shifting "Into the Zone" is a vital mental tool for success. Before now, most golfers can identify when they are "In the Zone" but I have never had a student who knew *how* to consistently move "Into the Zone." So this new technology is very exciting.

Use of the left brain to analyze the golf shot is important and then shifting to the right brain to execute the shot is how the golfer gets "Into the Zone." Practicing being in both states and identifying the uniqueness of how the states are different allows them to shift between the two states.

I have been working primarily with the FocusBand and have had incredible results with my students. They have really enjoyed working on the mental side and validating that the work they have been doing is helping them. They have all taken the Learning Assessments and spent time identifying their single cues. They have been disciplined in their practice and play to remain single focused and positive. And now with the FocusBand they can validate that they are staying focused and they are able to better "manage their brain." Their enjoyment of the game, their scoring, their shot and putting results, have all improved.

Myelination
Highly sophisticated computerized research on the golf swing and short game skills has been done in the last 20 years. The knowledge of the most efficient way to use the human body to hit a golf ball is now known. Look at the best golf swings on the Tour today and you will see great similarities—Rory McIlroy, Scott Adams, Jason Day, Jordan Spieth, Ricky Fowler. In the past professional golf swings were much more varied and personally unique—Jack Nicklaus, Lee Trevino, Arnold Palmer, Miller Barber, Gary Player. Today's professionals with more unique swings include Dustin

Johnson, Phil Mickelson, Jim Furyk, Tiger Woods. But unusual golf swings on today's professional tours are more rare.

What can we learn from this observation and evolution? First, even though some great golfers had different swings, their swings were repetitive. They successfully made a habit of their unique swing motions and played with those swings. Jim Furyk is such a great example of a golfer who stuck to his swing, refused to change and has had great success. When Jim is playing golf he is not thinking about his golf swing. He repeated it so many times that it is a habit and he trusts it.

In training golfers to learn or change their swing I have always encouraged them to practice with singular focus repetitions away from the golf ball to make the swing and changes faster and more permanent. Once the golf ball is introduced, the golfer's focus changes. The natural response of the golfer is to judge the outcome of where the ball goes when hitting balls. And yes, that feedback is important. But if a golfer is learning new physical motion, the learning process should be set up to repeat and evaluate how precise and accurate the physical motion was, not where the golf ball went. Practicing golf skills to create good motion habits is a separate and very different practice from hitting balls or playing. Golf instruction would be more effective if they were separated.

The inventors of the FocusBand, discussed earlier in this chapter, also created a computer program to train the golf swing away from the ball. The distribution company, Own My Swing™, markets and provides training for this computer product, The Myelinator™. As introduced in Chapter 3, building habits through repetition is myelination and The Myelinator™ was designed to help golfers learn golf skills. More information is available at www.powermentalgolf.com.

The evolution of golf training away from the golf ball has been gradually evolving. Video training, motion sensor devices like The Myelinator™, KVest®, GEARS, force plate measurement devices and robotic swing devices are all attempting to improve the physical side of training for golf.

Other sports are already using more efficient, singular focused training methods that train their athletes with more precise motion repetitions with feedback on success of learning those motions. They are creating opportunities for myelination of physical skills for those individual sports.

Good golf instructors know what golf swing mechanics to teach. The methods of best delivering that with integration with the mental game are the *future* good news for the game. When golf instructors are educated on the importance of teaching the researched knowledge of the physical *and* mental game and deliver it in the learning preferences of each student, learning and playing golf will be faster, easier and more fun.

Advanced Medical Technology: Electrical Medicine Products

I share with my students the following information regarding electrical medicine and products they can own to avoid and treat various injuries caused by playing golf.

Golfers develop injuries when practicing and playing, usually involving the various body joints including elbow, wrist, fingers, knees, back, shoulder, or ankle. Over the last 30 years I have studied the remedies to these joint issues and have learned about "electrical medicine treatment" for inflammation of the joints. Two products are particularly efficient for personal, at home or traveling treatment to alleviate those injuries. These products are FDA approved and available without prescription. I have been involved in the development of these products. I use these products and recommend them to my clients. The results have been excellent.

During the course of product development, I found this book: *The Body Electric: Electromagnetism and the Foundation of Life* by Robert Becker and Gary Selden. It is a fascinating book and explains the body's electrical system and how the body uses energy to heal itself.

To learn more about this book, visit The Power of Mental Golf *website:* *www.powermentalgolf.com*

Light Relief®

Light Relief® is a compact, handheld battery-powered device using an infrared light emitting diodes (LED) technology. It is painless, easy-to-use, and is designed to treat minor muscle pains, joint pains, stiffness, arthritis, muscle spasms, and other body pains.

To learn more about Light Relief®, visit The Power of Mental Golf website: www.powermentalgolf.com

Laser Touch One™

The LaserTouchOne™ is a pain relief device that combines **two proven therapies:** low level laser therapy and micro-current electrical stimulation which promotes the body's natural healing process at the cellular level. The device is a safe alternative to medication or surgery and can eliminate the need for costly prescriptions. It's painless, easy-to-use, and portable, so that pain relief is always in the palm of your hand.

To learn more about Laser Touch One™, visit The Power of Mental Golf website: www.powermentalgolf.com

CHAPTER 6

YOU ARE YOUR BEST COACH

"Be the Captain of Your Ship"
"Manage Your Brain"
"Use Single Cues"

You *CAN* play better golf.

But you need to take the information in this book and begin your journey to better learning, managing your brain, and having well-fit golf equipment. I am confident that many ideas in this book have your full attention and you know they are true. My students' intuition and their golf experience stories have proved to be my best encouragement to write this book. After applying the concepts in this book, their golf games improved, their fun in golf increased, and their lives were changed. Due to their improvement, I was moved to share this information with you.

Ninety-five percent of my students come to me with an unorganized thought process for their golf game. They are either thinking too many things or have random thoughts and distractions. One of the most-asked golf questions I have received through the years is, "What should I be thinking?" They often know that they are distracted and lacking in focus as they stand over the ball. Multi-track thinking has become commonplace in our world today and many golfers wrongly believe that they should multi-track think over the golf ball. The golf instruction and golf media industries have given them lots of information and encouraged them to use all that information in first learning and then seeking the perfect mechanical swing.

Golfers have been encouraged to think about many things over the ball "to get it right." Many golfers will try out every tip in the books, magazines, and on TV and take tips from their friends in their search for that perfect swing. Therefore, it is not a surprise that most golfers have many distracting thoughts and are often on the search for more tips. For the most part, golfers are very disorganized in their thinking and disoriented on the golf course. Therefore, they show up on my lesson tee asking, "What *should* I be thinking?"

When my students have golf clubs that do not fit them correctly, they usually *know* it.

They would rarely tell me that unless I asked and then they would tell it all. They could sense that a club was too long or too short or too heavy. I have found that golfers are smart and when asked their perceptions and experiences, their answers are often brilliant. But the golf club manufacturers, golf instruction industry, and golf media industry never let you believe that you should know such things. However, when my students hit a club that is properly fit for them, they can tell the difference right away and know that it is better for them.

So who is managing your brain? *You* have to. If these ideas resonated with you and your experiences, act on it. Begin to change your perceptions about your golf game. Begin to use the information, exercises, and tools offered in this book to practice and play differently. Talk about this with your friends. This will be a paradigm shift for you and friends, with more fun and success on the horizon. Yes, it will be a journey that may take some time to form new habits, but it will be interesting. I have seen hundreds of people change their perceptions almost overnight and then begin to create new habits of thinking and acting to own how they learn and how they process information. Go for it!!

FOCUS...
Use the Information in this book
To proceed on your journey
To learn how you learn and focus best...
And then do it!

Take an assessment of your golf clubs
And then proceed on your intuition!

Take Charge! Learning, Playing, Equipment, and Attitude

Learning

Find out how *you* learn. Take the Learning Assessment to assess your best way to learn golf. From information in the first two chapters you can learn your tendencies and how to begin to apply them to your golf game. Following the directions will help you apply the new skills.

This is also new knowledge for most golf instructors. If you have an instructor or are looking for an instructor, I recommend that you share the "Learning" information with an instructor that you like and ask her or him to help you integrate your unique golf learning styles to her or his instruction with you. You might even ask the golf instructor to take the Learning Assessment and then compare your learning styles with your instructor's. You will find that an instructor who matches your learning and processing style will probably be a better teacher for you—speaking to you in the language, images, rhythm, and feelings that you live in.

An instructor who *knows* how they learn and process information and understands that many others learn and process differently can be a good teacher for you because he or she can adapt to your style.

Playing

Here are a few thoughts as you begin a round...

Stay in the Present

Let go of the past, expectations, and any anger and frustration.

Don't get ahead of yourself by thinking about future holes or score.

Use your Golf Shot Routine, both mental and physical, that serves you, your timing, and your Learning Style.

Make the Golf Shot Routine a habit, both in Practice and Playing, so it becomes as natural as tying your shoes. Creating that habit is the secret to staying in the present at the most important times during your golf round—in those precious seconds while you are executing your shots.

Golf Equipment

Take the Golf Club Assessment on the Power Mental Golf website www.powermentalgolf.com

Consider getting a personal club fitting with the Blaisdell Company.

Study and learn more about equipment and how it fits you to help you make wise decisions when you purchase equipment. Consider investing in equipment that is fit for you....

Most important, pay attention to shaft flex, shaft length, grip size, lie angle, and club weight.

Attitude

Brain research has now proved that maintaining a positive attitude with positive thoughts will reinforce your imagination, your body/brain connection, your decision-making ability, your performance under pressure, and your short and long term consistency in your golf game. It is a major strategy to accomplish better golf success by making *Positive Thinking* a habit in practice and play.

CHAPTER 7

BE ONE OF THE
BEST INSTRUCTORS

There is always more to learn. I am glad that you are still reading and looking for more information about how to be a better golfer and/ or golf instructor.

This chapter is written for those who want to help others with their golf game—professional instructors, coaches, volunteers, parents and golfers with family and friends. The general public does not really know much about the state of the golf instruction industry. They assume that if a golf instructor is working at a golf club or driving range, they have had training to be a golf teacher, like a school teacher is required to be educated and certified to teach.

What Are the Facts on Golf Instructor Training?
Some golf professionals are well trained to be golf instructors and some are not. Golf instructors have three basic affiliations: LPGA, PGA of America, and non-affiliated. The Ladies Professional Golf Association (LPGA) does extensive training and specific golf instruction "Certification" of all their Teaching and Club Professional members. The Professional Golfers' Association of America (PGA of America) professionals provide golf instructor training through "on the job" experience and seminars. The PGA of America does not have any specific Teaching Certification. Non-affiliated golf teachers are primarily self-taught. While the LPGA

teachers are well trained and certified, they are a minority of active instructors in the golf industry. If you have an opportunity to have an LPGA instructor, odds are high that it will be a very good instruction experience. Qualified LPGA teachers can be found in your area through the www.LPGA.com website.

Golfers who take instruction are looking for only one of two things: to play better golf and/or to enjoy it more. They put their golf life in the hands of the instructor and are willing to do anything the instructor suggests to improve their golf game. The instructor has an important responsibility to enhance the self-esteem of the golfer during the process of golf instruction. If a teacher has not been trained in multiple instruction techniques and in the role of properly fit golf equipment, it is difficult to fulfill the responsibility of enhancing the self-esteem of the student. The student never says, "You have offended me and damaged my self-esteem." They just try hard and go away wondering why they did not do better. They often go away thinking that they are broken and not able to play this game. Often they quit the game of golf entirely. They never think that the golf instructor is wrong, partly because the golfing public believes that all golf instructors have been carefully trained to teach. In America, the education and training of instructors in most industries is very professional and provides instructor's certification. The golf consumer assumes that golf instructors have that same level of training and certification. Unfortunately, except for the LPGA certification program, that is just not true.

The majority of instructors believe that if they have excellence in golf "swing technique," they will be a good instructor. The majority of golf lessons today focus on the swing mechanics and technique of the swing or the short game. Of course, "physical swing technique" is important but it is only one part of the golf instructor's toolbox in teaching golf.

Excellence in golf instruction will evolve and become common-place when golf instructors:

- Identify their own learning preference.

- Assess each of their golf student's learning preference and adapt their teaching techniques to the individual student's learning preference.

- Assess each of their golf student's golf equipment and determine how well it compliments the student and performance.

- Have access to local and national resources that will manufacture golf equipment and make adjustments to clubs that are determined in proper club fittings.

- Integrate physical swing training with mental skills training.

In conclusion, when golf instructors are taught about the basic functioning of our brains, they will be able to help each student learn the physical motion and then guide them on how to get "In the Zone" on the course to perform at each person's highest level. These will be the goals of a golf instructor.

The outcome for golf students will be increased Confidence and Consistency.

Be Prepared

Below are the categories for study and excellence for those who would like to improve their teaching skills. A good instructor will have knowledge within these categories and will strive to communicate, as simply as he or she can, the tenets of each of these categories to the student. Simplicity is very important.

Golf Instruction Mastery Skill Categories

1. The skills of assessment, observation, and minimal verbal instruction

2. Understanding and identifying Sensory System Strengths of the instructor and golf students

3. Understanding and identifying Brain Hemispheric processing preferences of the instructor and golf students

4. Knowing how to guide each student to use his or her brain in the left and right side at the appropriate times in practicing and playing golf

5. Communicating with each student in the terms of how each learns

6. Assessment of client's past injury and avoidance of future injury

7. Ball Flight Laws based on the Laws of Physics

8. Golf Equipment—both the physics and the design—and how equipment affects the golf shot, chip, or putt

9. Full Swing Dynamics, based on physiology and physics

10. Short Game Dynamics: Chipping, Sand, and Putting

11. Physiology, Stretching, Strengthening

12. Appropriate use of video technology, computer analysis technology, learning tools and drills based on the student's learning styles and preferences

13. Golf Course Management for each player's game

14. Emotional Management Strategies

15. Instruction for the physically, emotionally, or mentally challenged

16. Understanding child development to make the instruction appropriate to the golfer's age

17. Knowledge and experience in using portable EEG machines to train brain management

18. Emphasis on enhancing the self-esteem of every student

You don't have to be an *expert* in every field, but the more information and application you can learn about each one, the more effective you will be. Stay open to continued learning through reading, attending seminars, and conversing with other golf instructors and sports training resources.

Focus more time on learning all 15 aspects rather than just the golf swing techniques to be a more effective and well-rounded golf instructor.

Of course, as an instructor, you will always learn from each and every teaching experience that you have.

Resources
Besides reading, attending training sessions, observing other instructors, and participating in ongoing conversation with other instructors, I highly recommend that you find local resources for yourself and your students in as many of these categories as possible.

Those resources should include the following:

- a Club Fitting expert
- a Sports Physical Therapist with experience in golf
- a stretching expert with experience in golf
- a Sports Medicine Doctor with experience in golf
- an expert in mental aspects of golf
- a Strength Trainer with golf training experience

First Learn, then Teach
You need to have self-knowledge about *your* golf game in as many of the categories listed above in order to facilitate the learning of your golf students.

Absorbing this book is a good start to expand your horizons. It is important for you, as a teacher, to know your strengths and weaknesses. You need to know your own Learning Style, Brain Processing preference, and Sensory System strengths and weaknesses. Be sure to take the Learning Assessment and identify your preferences. When teaching golf, it is important for you, as the instructor, to know how both you and your student prefer to learn and process information and for you to be able to deliver the information in the way that the student best understands. The instructor needs to get into the world of the student rather than expect the student to move into the instructor's world.

I have observed (and have been told about) many lessons in which the golf students were absolutely lost during the instruction because it did not make any sense to them. The instructor was presenting information through the lens of her or his own learning and processing preference and the presentation did not fit the golf student's learning preference. In those cases, the student and instructor were in different learning worlds. Unfortunately, students most often go away from an experience like that thinking that they failed, are broken, or are not athletic enough for golf. Too often the instructor tends to agree with that assessment about the student.

Untrained instructors are often not sure why the student is failing to learn and improve because they just don't know any better. The instructor believes that there is something wrong with the student. There is a common perception among golf instructors and in the golf industry that golf is a difficult game and many people just can't learn to play well or get any better. That belief is not true. If the student is failing to learn, the instructor needs to take the responsibility for that failure and either find a way to communicate better or recommend an instructor who may be a better fit for the student.

Golf students have more success when the instructor can present instruction in the way that fits the student's learning preference. It would be a far better experience for the golf student and for the growth of the game of golf if golf instructors would take responsibility to improve their instruction skills in the area of learning styles with the goal of providing a better golf education experience.

An instructor does not have to be a great player to teach the game of golf, but the instructor has to be an educated, informed, and self-knowledgeable golfer in the categories defined above to be a good instructor.

The majority of golf instructors have not been trained sufficiently in the areas of learning styles and club fitting. Seldom will the student tell them directly that they are dissatisfied, because most golf students have not experienced a lesson from a well-trained golf instructor. Until they experience a much better lesson, they do not know what a really good golf lesson is like—a lesson that's delivered in their learning style with consideration of their equipment and all the items on the above list.

I call it the "black hole"—a gap that exists between an eager golf student and a teacher who is not sufficiently trained to teach. The instructor has plenty to say and demonstrate and the golf student is eager to learn. Neither the student or the teacher can identify it, but the "black hole" is the place into which the instructor's information is going because it is not pertinent, not delivered in the student's learning preference, contains too much information, or is just wrong and irrelevant information. Also into the "black hole" goes the student's self-confidence, self-esteem, and joy in the learning process. Besides the damage to the self-esteem of the student, the self-esteem of the instructor is damaged as well.

How can a Lesson of Excellence be identified? The student should become better while on the lesson tee or in the short game area. The student should be getting better with every instruction session and then gradually be able to take what he or she has learned to the course with confidence and consistency.

Too often in the current golf instruction model, the student does not improve during the lesson. They may have hit a few good shots or in some cases, become worse. At the end of these failed lessons, the instructor will often say, "Just keeping working on it and it will get better." However, for those students, it most often does *not* get better when they leave the lesson tee and 'work on it' because the instruction session was flawed.

The Power of Taking a Risk
Teaching is an art. The more caring and supportive you are as a teacher, the better your result will be. The more training you have in all aspects of teaching golf, the better your result will be. Begin by assessing your level of excellence in the areas of learning, club fitting, and the additional categories on the list that were presented earlier in this chapter. By learning more about how you learn, how others learn, and how to get into *their* world, your instruction success will increase. The more you know about how golf equipment affects the golf shot, the more consistently your student will hit the ball. Put the learning knowledge and the right equipment together and you will increase your magic. We are all different and the more we can understand our differences, the more we can empower ourselves and others.

It is especially important for college coaches to learn about themselves and each of their players. Each player is different and will have a better college experience if the coach can understand the unique world the athlete brings with them to the golf team.

Giving "Tips" and Helping Friends

One of the most damaging activities I see golfers do is to give golf advice to their friends, family —and even strangers—especially when they're on the golf course. I'm not sure why or how this behavior became acceptable. What I do know, because I have observed it over and over again, is that giving tips causes great distraction. The golfer giving the tip is probably genuinely trying to help and probably cares for the person they are "tipping." The result for the recipient is usually chaos in their brain organization as they now add that "tip" to all they were already thinking about. It's a distraction and usually causes bad shots.

I have had hundreds of golfers express their frustration with all the tips and recommendations they get from other golfers. They want to be polite with their friends and family, so they act as if it's OK. But it's not OK. It rarely helps them. It hurts them and they just don't want to appear to be rude by asking their friends and family to stop. And when I hear about strangers approaching golfers on the driving range or on the course with "tips," it amazes me. You would not walk into someone's home or office and begin to rearrange the décor or give them "tips" on better home or work management without being asked for that advice.

Unless you know how you and the other individual learn and process information, you need to be very careful about giving advice and tips. Leave other golfers to their own thoughts and organization. Just because you heard it on The Golf Channel, or because the "tip" works for you, does not mean it will work for your friend. Golf instruction and tips need to be presented in an organized fashion and fit into the fabric of the golfer's belief systems and learning styles. Swing Instruction should be limited to the driving range or away from the ball. Instruction on the course should be focused on rules or course management.

The Power of Mental Golf System Workbook can be accessed online at www.powermentalgolf.com. This workbook is structured to allow a golf instructor to assess the level of their skills and set goals to improve in the various categories. There are resources listed in the workbook that can be used to improve your teaching knowledge and effectiveness.

CHAPTER 8

LEARNING WITH THE TOUR PROS

As we watch professional golfers play, compete, win, and lose, there is a great deal we can all learn. Any professional, woman or man, who makes it to the professional tour level is unquestionably an elite athlete. The difference between winning and not winning is undoubtedly a mental function—based on excellence in focus, relaxation, consistency, and confidence. Any professional who has won a tournament will testify to the truth of that statement. Players who win many tournaments and Major Tournaments know themselves pretty well and have recognized their unique skills. Many spend time practicing how they achieve and maintain their focus, relaxation, consistency, and confidence. They win when they do an especially good job of managing those skills when the stakes are high and when they are under high levels of pressure.

When a golfer senses the increasing pressure during competition, the body and brain start demonstrating different behaviors. The reactions are similar to the reaction of a human being under any threatening situation. That reaction has been defined as "stress." When the stress begins to occur, the human brain doesn't immediately know if the pressure is coming from trying to play well and win a golf tournament or if they are actually experiencing a real threat to the human being's survival. The heart beats faster, the brain is more easily distracted, and all the mechanisms of flight for survival activate. That reaction has been defined as "fight or flight."

To the brain and body, it is real. It is triggered by thoughts in the brain and by past experiences that are held in memory. What winners learn to do is recognize their reactions to pressure and learn what unique strategies they can employ that work for them under that pressure. Every person reacts differently to this experience and every person's strategy to maintain the focus, relaxation, consistency, and confidence will be different.

The difference in the strategies employed by the golfer to deal with pressure will be dependent on what the unique learning system of the individual is and how well trained or experienced they are in keeping the left brain quiet and the right brain appropriately creative during shot execution. Everyone will do it a little differently. As a golf instructor, I cannot immediately tell golfers what strategies are right for them. Rather, I use the Learning Assessment and then a hitting session with meaningful questioning, to help guide them to identify 'how they will focus best.' Each person has a unique way to focus. An instructor should guide the student to "discover" what he or she does naturally to focus and apply that to golf, and encourage each to practice her or his focus on every shot.

If you want to maintain a better game under pressure, first take the Learning Assessment to learn your natural learning style and brain processing preference and check out the tendencies of golfers with your similar styles and preferences as outlined in Chapter 1. Then, follow the instructions in Chapter 2 to explore your own learning system, learning as much as you can about yourself. Set some strategies to deal with focus and pressure and then practice those on the range and on the course. Once you have discovered more about yourself, you will find that you can create consistent reactions to manage the pressure situations. When you find a good focus strategy that works for you to deal with those pressure situations, you will be more confident and consistent.

In addition, as Chapter 4 explains, your consistency in results and, therefore, confidence also depends upon how well your golf equipment fits you.

The focus of this book is on two factors: Identifying your mental strengths and being sure that your golf equipment is right for you.

Below are some observations of focus and equipment of golf professionals that you can see in person at tournaments or on TV. Have fun watching for their focus and equipment fits.

Women's Golf and LPGA Professionals

In America, 25% of golfers are women. Similar percentages exist at the junior golf level. It is important to attract more girls and women to play golf. Golf and the golf industry has been a male-dominated industry. Research over the last 20 years indicates a sense of exclusion and intimidation toward women. Most importantly, research shows that more women would play golf if they found the golf environment more inviting to women. A number of strategies, including better golf instruction and club fitting, and improved women-friendly training for golf club employees could help attract, train and retain women golfers.

In 1989, I helped launch the LPGA Girls Golf Club to create a better culture of development for girls in golf. That club is now the LPGA-USGA Girls Golf Club and has thousands of members and alumni who have learned the game, nurtured their skills, and supported each other to keep golf in their lives forever.

In 1991, 1993 and 1995, I led the LPGA, as National President, to host the first Women's Golf Summits. The conferences were each attended by over 400 industry leaders with growth of the women's game as the intended outcome. The Women's Summit series was successful in opening conversations about women's golf and encouraging the support of junior and women's golf programs. Continued research and open conversations about women's golf are important.

As for any golfer, club fitting for the women amateurs and professionals is vital. While a problem for taller male professionals is getting longer irons, this is not a common problem for the women professionals. Only a small number of women professionals are over 5'10"in height, so fulfilling the needs of the length of the club with proper swing weight for the majority of the women professional players is very achievable. However, the length of amateur women's irons is a problem. Golf club manufacturers have been making a standard length women's club and a petite women's length club for the last 40 years. A large percentage of amateur women are playing with clubs that are too short for their body specifications. If a woman is over 5'4" odds are high that her irons are too short. The taller the woman is, the higher the odds that her clubs are too short. Some taller women are using men's clubs. That will give them more length, but usually higher overall weight and swing weight. Even though a woman is taller, she is rarely as strong in her upper body as a male of the same height. Women in this situation should read Chapter 4 and follow the recommendations.

The more common golf club misfit for women professionals is the shaft flex. Golf manufacturers have traditionally fit strong women golfers with shaft flexes that are too stiff. With the new computers today, especially TrackMan technology, the measuring of club shafts for the women professionals has improved. But there are many junior, college, and some professional women players who do not have access to the best equipment and fitting technology. The golf industry has established a pattern to have good women players use very stiff shafts and very low loft drivers. There are a few LPGA Tour Players who are beginning to use softer flex shafts—Regular rather than Stiff or Extra Stiff—and hitting drivers with more driver loft, moving from around 8.0 degrees to 9.5 and 10.5 degrees. The better computer and TrackMan equipment is showing them that the launch angle and spin ratios can sometimes be better with softer shafts and more driver loft, resulting in longer drives and more accuracy.

Using technology for club fitting validation and research is important. However, for the golfer who wants to play and perform, getting too technical is usually a distraction. I recommend to golf instructors and club fitters that they be well versed in whatever technology they are using. Then, keep it simple for the golf student. The student may be curious, but all they really want is information to hit better shots and score better. Give them the most important information within their learning style to help keep them stay focused and maintain clarity. The golf instructor who gives their students voluminous information is doing the student a disservice. Many golf instructors think they look smart and are earning their fee by giving excessive information that just confuses the student. Golf instructors are the guides for their students and need to be the filter and be responsible for the information that they give them. Keep it simple and help keep them focused and clear.

Annika Sorenstam

Annika had a clear and simple focus for her golf shots. Her clubs were well fit and she was most often "In the Zone." When Annika would be off her game, she would have her caddy and coaches check her set-up and ball position. When she had the set-up and ball position at address correct, she played her best golf. She rarely worked on swing mechanics and her on-course focus was clear and consistent. She was coached by Pia Nilsson and Lynn Marriott to keep that focus. She is one of the best players ever and the golf world honors her and misses her.

Michelle Wie

What an incredible talent Michelle is. Unfortunately, because of her height, her irons have never been long enough for her. As is often the case with misfit irons, the body is put in stressed positions in hitting shots through all the practice sessions and competitive rounds. It shows up in back injuries, hip, knee, and ankle problems. With Michelle, her putting issues have been aggravated by her height. But she is smart and found a way to compensate in the swing and putting. With a better iron fit she could relieve the stress on her body and continue playing great golf.

Lydia Ko

What can we say about Lydia Ko... except WOW!! I was at the LPGA dinner when Lydia received the Rookie of the Year Award for 2014. She had captured the attention of the media and the entire LPGA with an incredible year of wins and records. She gave a wonderful speech, sharing with all of us her joy and gratitude. Lydia is a winner, a leader, and a joyful person.

I do not know how Lydia focuses, but I know that she does focus. In her second year, she was a bit distracted—like most players who have experienced incredible success. In closing 2015, she showed the strength of her exceptional athletic and golf skills. She is one of the leading LPGA players and will be for many years. She has a great swing, a strong ability to focus and play under pressure, stay present, and enjoy the moment.

PGA Tour Players

Tiger Woods
When Tiger had some personal problems and physical challenges, he seemed to have lost his high level of confidence and consistency. He began to take in lots of golf swing information and seems to have lost his right brain playing focus on the course. When he misses a shot he blames his golf swing and that left-brain thinking has become a habit. When he goes to the next shot, thinking about his golf swing mechanics, he is creating a state of distraction. Whenever a golfer starts working on changes in his or her physical golf swing, it takes time to make those changes a habit. Until the changes become a habit, thinking about them when under pressure will be a distraction. Hopefully Tiger will return to the Tour and hopefully he will return with good focus.

I suggest two strategies to use when making physical changes to your swing or short game:

1. Practice the Physical Change
Clarify what swing change(s) you want to make and spend time every day for up to a month just repeating those moves, away from the ball, for 15 to 30 minutes every day. Set a date when you think the change will have become habit. People are different,

but research has shown that repeating a move every day for 20 to 30 days will instill the habit to memory. After a month or two of continued practice repetitions away from the ball, those new habits will hold up under pressure.

2. Practice Your Focus

Practice hitting balls both on the range and on the course with the discipline of keeping your unique focus over the ball, as discussed in Chapter 1 and 2. Once the habit of the physical change is completed as described above, practice on the range and on the course with your focus. Be disciplined to not go back to several golf swing thoughts when over the ball. If those golf swing mechanics thoughts jump into your thought pattern on the course or when practicing, take a rehearsal swing and let them go. Go back to your single-focus image when executing the shot. That will create the habit of focus that you will need under pressure.

Rory McIlroy

Rory made some swing changes and changed his body and strength by diligently working out. Those changes have become habit now and his performance should be consistent if he remains disciplined and focused.

When watching Rory, I encourage you to note two parts of his swing that are exceptional that you might want to mimic in your swing. One: His great balance. He starts well and finishes well with incredible balance, especially in the follow through. And two: The rotation of his hips and core through the hit. Because his balance is so good, when he turns and clears his hips through the shot, it is really exceptional. There is no slide in his body motion through the hit.

Rory has let distractions cause him to occasionally have bad shots and high scores in Major Championships. But it appears that he has improved in identifying the strategies to play under the pressure and stress and to keep his focus and reduce distractions. As he improves his ability to do this and makes his focus a consistent habit, his consistency and confidence should bring him many more wins.

Ricki Fowler

Ricki Fowler made swing changes in the last two years. Similar to the results of Rory's changes, Ricki's swing changes produced a more compact arm swing and a powerful core body turn, and all done in excellent balance. His confidence is growing and his performance in 2015 has greatly improved. In 2015, he had a great mental breakthrough in winning the Players' Championship by keeping his focus through the full four rounds. He is one of the most popular young players and it is most likely that he will continue to grow to be one of the better players of his age group.

Jason Day

While Jason has played well on the PGA Tour, he has struggled to win major tournaments. Many times in the last five years he finished 2nd and many times in the top 5 in major events. In August of 2015, Jason broke through and won the PGA Championship, his first Major Championship. In the next 7 months, Jason won 6 tournaments, dominated in winning the 2016 Player's Championship and earned the #1 world ranking. It was obvious that Jason was in good focus. He was taking time as he prepared for each shot to stand behind the ball and close his eyes in focus before he approached the ball to execute the shot. Only Jason knows what he is imaging before he hits those shots, but it seems that he has found his focus.

For Jason, this is an especially important discovery. As a youngster, Jason had personal challenges after his father died and he has been very open about the emotional stress he had experienced and how it seemed to bother him when under pressure in trying to win those most important tournaments. Now that he seems to have found his focus, he should be able to fulfill his potential and dreams as a successful professional golfer.

Dustin Johnson

Dustin is one of the most powerful athletic players in the game today. His athletic ability and strength can give him an edge on the course.

Distractions on and off the course have sometimes presented a challenge for Dustin, interfering with his focus. While he has finished poorly in a number of important tournaments, there is no doubt that if he can identify his distractions and his reactions to stress, he could find his unique focus and keep that through the pressure rounds. With focus, he could be a dominant player on the tour.

Another observation that could help Dustin be even better is to test playing with irons that are longer, allowing him to set up in a more athletic position at address. His current irons are short for his height and body style. The woods, being naturally longer, are easier for him to hit with balance and consistency. On some shots, primarily irons, Dustin loses the athletic hip angle because he has to rise up a bit during the backswing to maintain his best balance and athletic power and then move slightly down through impact to retain the same distance from the ball.

Club fitting research has proven that a golfer's swing pattern is formed more from their iron swing than their wood swing. For most players, the woods are long enough that even the taller players can set up and swing in a taller, athletic position. But if the irons are too short, the taller player will set up in a less athletic position, with too much knee bend or spine angle or crouching at address. During the swing that golfer will look for better balance in the backswing and follow through which will cause an up and down motion in the swing, i.e. Charles Barkley's swing. Timing that up and down motion with the core body rotation on the iron swings adds another complication and can easily cause poor shots, especially under pressure. But then when they set up with their driver, they do not have to make the compensations in the set-up or the swing and therefore their iron and wood set up and swings will often be different. Having different set ups and swings can contribute to inconsistency and loss of confidence.

Dustin and the three players named below are excellent examples of players whose irons are too short for them. The golf industry has not provided longer clubs to fit taller people because with the traditional weighting of the iron club heads, the swing weights get too heavy as the club shaft gets longer. However in the last few years, we have worked diligently to get manufacturers to provide longer clubs built with appropriate swing weights for taller people (and for golfers with longer legs and higher hips).

Gary Blaisdell, founder of Blaisdell Performance Systems, works with major manufacturers to build longer, lighter clubs to fit the taller man and woman golfer. You may want to review Chapter 4 for more information on club fitting.

Bubba Watson
Bubba is a natural and committed golfer. He knows his swing and believes in his abilities. He will be wise to keep his natural swing. Bubba plays golf, not golf swing!!

As I described above, his iron length causes him to be in a less athletic and balanced position at address. If he had better balance at address with longer shafts in his irons, it would help him maintain his balance and power throughout the swing. When watching Bubba, you might note how off balance he occasionally seems in his follow through position due partially to clubs that are too short for his body type.

Matt Kuchar
Matt is a wise athlete and golfer. At some point in his career he realized that swinging the club on a traditional swing plane was not very effective for him. He practiced in a room with a low ceiling so he would lower his swing plane. Whether he realized it or not, he had to do this because his irons were too short for his height. By lowering his swing plane below his shoulders, he was able to minimize the sense of moving up and down to compensate for the short length of the iron and to hit the ball. With that lower swing plane, he can execute his turn without timing an additional up and down move. Because he is such a good athlete, he is most often able to maintain his balance throughout the swing, but it is sometimes a little off balance in his finish position because of that lower swing plane.

Matt is a great ambassador for the game of golf. Adding length to his irons could allow him better balance, contribute to increased consistency, and save his back in the long term.

Keegan Bradley

Keegan's irons are also too short for him. In his set up with his irons he has a deep knee bend and crouch with his upper body. That makes keeping his athletic balance through the swing difficult. But like the other great tour players, his elite athletic ability and determination allows him to fight for and keep his balance most of the time. He is such a rhythm player that if he gets his rhythm focus, he can make the shots happen and, with longer iron shafts, he could be even more awesome. A situation that can be very difficult for players with clubs that are too short is shots on uneven lies. It is even more difficult to keep balance on uneven lies if the set up is not tall and athletic.

All of the professional golfers above are superior athletes and have demonstrated by their success that they understand the tremendous importance of the mental aspect of the game. All have different physical attributes and have mastered their own way to focus on the course. When they win they have been a master of focus that week. If the golf club allows the athlete to set up tall and in an athletic position, the natural physical golf swing would be easier to repeat and add to consistency and confidence.

As you watch the tour events as a spectator on site or on TV, observe the body build, height, and leg length of the professionals and compare the players that are under 5'11" and over 5'11" and the players who have long legs and a short torso. You will see a major difference in their set up position with their irons. The taller players will have more knee flex and lean over more at address. It is much more difficult for the taller or longer-leg player to achieve and maintain athletic balance through the swing. They have to move up and down or extremely adjust their swing plane to stay stable. Just check it out—I think you'll be amazed at what you'll see... and learn.

Charles Barkley and Michael Jordan

Message to Charles and Michael: call us! You are the epitome of elite athletes and as is the case with so many great athletes, you are both tall. While the golf industry has not focused on properly fitting tall people, we can fit you for longer golf clubs that would turn your golf game around immediately and make you both more successful and happier golfers.

Check in with us at www.powermentalgolf.com. Or call us to set up a magic club fitting that will change your golf lives.

CHAPTER 9

BUT... WHAT ABOUT SWING MECHANICS?

The main focus of this book has been the mental aspects of learning and playing golf and the importance of properly fit golf equipment. So what about Swing Mechanics?

Concentration in golf instruction has been focused primarily on the mechanics of the golf swing. Swing mechanics is physical motion of the body moving while swinging the golf club and creating power delivered through the golf club to the ball. For more than a century, before video and computer analysis, golfers played following their best instincts on how to deliver power and accuracy from swinging the golf club to and through the ball. And golf instructors facilitated the golfer's belief that having better or perfect swings would create better shots and better scores.

Are swing mechanics important? Yes, they are. They are, of course, part of learning "how to swing the golf club." Every golfer has a golf swing. And every person has "swing mechanics" that make up that golf swing. Some learn the swing in their own way and some take instruction to learn or improve their swing. Golf instructors have a responsibility to understand the most advanced metrics of the golf swing and then be able to communicate that in a simple way to each student, fulfilling their individual needs.

There has been extensive research for years on which "swing mechanics" are best—to provide power and accuracy. In the last few years, with the most modern computer and motion sensor technology, the use of sensors, motion measuring devices and club component and ball speed measurement devices, the most efficient movement of the human body in the golf swing and the results in creating power and efficiency in ball striking has been measured. From all that technology and research the "most efficient" golf swing has been defined—with the measurement of positions, angles, motion sequence of various parts of the body, weight transfer, and video graphics of body motion. The "best" golf swing for the ideal human body with ideal golf equipment has been defined and is available for instructors and golfers to review.

All this information needs to be simplified so that the golfer can learn quickly and correctly. Some instructors have created a simplification and that kind of simplification needs to become an industry wide training. Defining each person's learning style and adapting computer technology will help. It is the future of all sports training and when the golf industry embraces that combination, golf will be easier to learn and play with proficiency.

The "belief system" of golfers, instructors, and the golf industry needs to be examined in regards to golf instruction and learning the golf swing and game of golf.

A good case can be made that integration of the mental and physical aspects of learning the golf swing and how to play the game of golf should happen and that would enhance the skills, increase in accomplishment and fun for golfers. It probably will contribute to the growth of the game of golf.

These are the questions players, golf instructors, and the golf industry need to consider to accomplish the integration of the physical and mental aspects in golf instruction and playing the game.

1. What is the best way to teach the positions and motion of the golf swing?

2. How does the golfer with less-than-ideal athletic body adapt the *best* swing to fit his or her body?

3. How can a person learn the golf swing that is not perfect, but best for them, accept that swing, and then move on and be done with the basics of golf swing learning?

4. How does the golfer know when he or she has arrived at the point when the golf swing has become a habit and becomes as natural as tying one's shoes?

5. Can a golfer ever be *done* with their golf swing and then *play* golf rather than *playing "Fix the Golf Swing?"*

6. What does the golfer want to learn after the golf "skills" learning is done?

These are provocative questions for today's golfers, instructors, and the golf industry.

By understanding how human beings learn, applying instruction techniques that speed the learning and convert that learning to habit in a short period of time, the answers to the above questions can become part of a new belief system of golfers and instructors.

My experience has proved that the answer to #5 is YES—a golfer can and should be done at some point with their golf swing and then *play* golf rather than *playing "Fix the Golf Swing?"* The answer to #6 is to learn to play with mental confidence and consistency.

It is my responsibility as a golf instructor to guide a student to develop the belief that they can get to that point and then help them get there.

After that, there may be minor tweaks or adjustments to set-up, ball placement, and balance, but the golf swing will remain basically the same, if it was learned appropriately with properly fit golf equipment. Improvement in the joy of the game then comes from mental improvement.

Recommendations for Learning and Teaching Golf

First, assess these eight important factors:
1. The student's goals and motivations for playing golf and taking instruction.

2. Physical factors: the individual's flexibility, strength, balance, body shape, age, left or right hand preferences, eye dominance, injury history and any unique physical concerns by the student.

3. The learning preferences of the student, measured by the Learning Assessment.

4. The student's golf swing and short game skills.

5. The time the student has available and will commit to practice, at home and at the course.

6. The student's golf equipment and how well it is fit to the student.

7. The student's golf course management skills. This is best assessed on the course.

8. The student's belief systems about what creates ball flight, the best golf swing for them, their own confidence and other beliefs that can affect their learning and performance. Some of these beliefs may be assessed in the first instruction sessions facilitated by the instructor asking relevant questions. And many beliefs will surface during the follow up instruction sessions. The instructor wants to always be checking with the student on their beliefs. Creating congruency between the beliefs and the instruction will facilitate faster and more effective learning, ball striking and performance on the course.

After assessing the individual's current golf game, based on the above eight factors, the golf instructor must make a decision on the path to take to assist the golfer. That path includes prioritizing the following...

The Phases of Learning
1. Recognizing learning preferences
2. Physical Skill Training for all parts of the game
3. Setting goals for sufficient repetition to myelinate (make habit) the desired physical skills
4. Guiding the student to *own* the motion after repetition and myelination
5. Guiding the student to learn to Practice and Play "In the Zone"
6. On course management of decision making and creating the "Zone" for every shot.

Teaching Basics and Order Priority
Before or after the very first lesson, the Learning Assessment should be administered.

The preferred skill training sequence is to teach putting first, chipping second, full swing third and course management fourth. This sequence is especially important for beginners and can be adjusted for experienced golfers.

Throughout the learning process the mental management aspects as defined in the Learning Assessment should be used to consistently guide the instruction.

Basic Golf Skills

Putting
1. Set Up
2. Compact stroke – Hit and Hold
3. Balance
4. Read pace first and then read break

Chipping System Basics
1. Set Up
2. Grip (Same as swing grip)
3. Chip Style Selection:
   a. Chip and Run
   b. Lofted Chip
   c. Cut Shot
   d. Seve Ballesteros Shot and Cut Shot
   e. Mini Golf Swing
4. Practice specific distances

Sand Game Basics
1. Greenside bunker
2. Fairway bunker

Golf Swing Basics
1. Balance at Address and Follow Through
2. Address Position: Grip, lower body and upper body position
3. Follow Through Position
4. Lower Body: Feet, legs, hips, weight transfer
5. Upper Body: Core rotation with club in plane / transition position / plane
6. Sequence of motion (kinematic sequence)

**Tips For Integrating Learning Swing Mechanics
with Learning to Be "In the Zone"**

For the Golfer:
1. Focus on only one task at a time.

2. When working with an instructor, ask the instructor to keep the focus on one piece of learning at a time and keep the instruction and cues to singular focus. The brain can best learn with a single focus cue and repetitions.

3. Work on one skill development with daily repetitions for three weeks. Practice the skill away from hitting balls to best train the new motion. When hitting balls during that three-week period, hit with only one focus for each shot. Singular focus and repetitions on the skill you want to learn will create the fastest learning for that skill.

4. To speed up your learning, use your preferred learning style—visual, auditory, tactile, or kinesthetic...and right or left brain. Follow the guides in this book to enhance your learning speed and efficiency.

For the Golf Instructor:

1. Learn *your* Learning Preference and how that relates to your golf game and how you teach.

2. Learn each student's Learning Preference and approach all learning with that in mind.

3. Every lesson should have a specific purpose and goal. At every lesson, try to determine what the student wants most to accomplish and set a path to deliver that.

4 Practice your observation skills of the motor skills of the student's swing and short game skills. Decide where to start and set a path for instruction.

5. During the lesson, work on a single mental cue and if appropriate, a single physical cue.

6. Progress during the lesson is imperative. Your student should make progress in understanding and skill development while he/she is with you.

7. The instructor's responsibility is to deliver to the student the help to improve his or her golf skills, both mental and physical. It is also the instructor's responsibility to ensure that the student can take the skills learned in the practice areas successfully onto the golf course.

8. The primary goal of the golf instructor is to assist the golfer in reaching their golf goals through understanding the student's goals, learning preferences, instructing with the best knowledge on the physical and mental aspects of golf. The second major goal is to create a learning environment and training techniques that will allow the student to learn the mental skills, the physical swing and golf shot skills so that they become habit. The third goal is to work to constantly enhance the self-esteem of the student.

POWER MENTAL GOLF WORKBOOKS
based on the information in this book
can be accessed online at www.powermentalgolf.com
The Golfer Workbook
The Golf Instructor Workbook

CASE STUDIES
of Individual Clients

I recommend to all golfers and golf instructors that they use the PMG System detailed in this book to improve their confidence and consistency. Below are stories of clients who have followed this system.

"The golf students and their stories are real.
Their names have been changed to protect the innocent and the guilty."

Jackson   Golf Professional • 27 years old

Learning Preference: Equal Kinesthetic/Tactile primary with high secondary Visual. Left Brain Dominant with a strong Right brain score.

Sensory Cues: His cues, based in the K/T sensory system, helped him create a calm, more relaxed state. For him, imagining being at the beach and the relaxed feel in his hands and left arm are important to being "In The Zone." He visualizes the ball flight path from behind the ball as he relaxes and when over the ball, keeps the feeling of relaxation in his hands and left arm.

Physical Swing work: Jackson shortened his backswing and improved the loading in the backswing with hip turn and posting weight onto his right leg. Then he improved the turn through the ball. He worked on one skill at a time. He committed to a single swing cue during the time of his swing changes and committed to a single focus as a picture of that single change. Once his swing changes were completed and become habit, he no longer had to think about any swing mechanics. His cues became visual and tactile/kinesthetic, as described above.

Club Fitting: His entire set was evaluated. His wedges were too upright and Lie Angle Adjustments were made to the three wedges. He purchased a new driver with similar shaft and one-half degree less loft.

FocusBand: From his initial use of the FocusBand, the feedback validated for him that he was managing his brain as he had practiced, using the left brain when analyzing the shot and using the right brain to hit the shot. When he was not "In The Zone" due to internal or external distraction, the feedback told him he was in the left brain. He practiced away from the ball and in practice on and off the course to have focus in the left and right brain at the appropriate times.

Outcome: After one year of work and 6 weeks of using the FocusBand, he felt an increase in confidence and consistency in practice and play. His scores lowered, his putting improved and anxious feelings lessened when in pressure situations.

Electrical Medical: Jackson used Light Relief® and Laser Touch One™ for shoulder injury and thumb inflammation.

Patricia   Amateur Golfer • 23 Handicap • 40 years old

Learning Preference: Visual/Auditory primary and high Tactile secondary. She is slightly left-brain dominant with a secondary strong right brain preference.

Sensory Cues: To get relaxed, she plays songs or tunes in her mind. Her favorite visual cue is the target where she wants the ball to go. Then, she walks into the ball the same way each time, carrying the club in the left hand, keeping it relaxed and walking with a rhythm. As soon as she is set, she continues the rhythm through the swing.

Physical Swing Work: She focuses on a balanced start and finish. Patricia took lessons for over a year from a strong left brain analytical instructor. Before that instruction, she played golf for many years in a right brain natural way and then when influenced by the year of instruction from the left brain instructor, she started over thinking and analyzing every physical part of the swing. Due to the left-brain instruction, her lifelong swing was blocked and as a result her anxiety level when on the course had overcome her game. Over the year of left brain instruction, she went from shooting in the low 90s to shooting in the 120s. We worked together to rediscover her old physical swing and the mental state she had played with for many years, before the intense left-brain instruction had taken her away from her natural right brain game.

Club Fitting: We evaluated her clubs and found that they were well fit. She is still searching for a putter that helps her recapture the right brain sense of calmness and connection that she played with before changing both her putter and putting style in the last year of instruction.

FocusBand: She first practiced with the FocusBand in indoor sessions, both sitting, walking, and putting. She initially discovered that she was operating in a very left brain, analytical style. As she practiced and received the feedback from the FocusBand, she began to discover how to shift to her right brain, returning more to the style she had used before the influence of the left-brain instruction.

After learning to make the shift to the right brain, she practiced swinging her driver and then hitting balls. She became aware very quickly of when she was in her left brain, caused by over analytical and negative thinking. Within a few days she began to experience success on the course using the right brain focus approach over the ball. Using the FocusBand, she was able to validate that using her Tactile and Visual favorite cues kept her in the correct brain performance mode.

Outcome: During our FocusBand instruction, she improved dramatically after identifying her visual and tactile learning preferences. She began using that right brain focus to replace the left brain "constant analysis, and swing thoughts." Using the FocusBand validated that when she was in the calm and focused state, she had been able to switch to the right brain side. She began to hit better shots and improve her confidence and consistency. After four weeks of FocusBand practice, her scores moved into the 90s and continue to improve.

Jennifer   Business Executive • 22 Handicap • 45 years old

Learning Preference: Tactile primary and Visual secondary. Right Brain Preference

Sensory Cues: Sensing peace and relaxation by breathing before approaching the ball. Seeing the target and keeping the quiet sense of peace and relaxation setting up and then hitting. Keeping internally quiet is important for her to keep the sense of peace and relaxation.

Physical Swing Work: She focuses on a more complete shoulder rotation in her backswing and better posting onto her right side. To make these a habit, she began by learning these skills away from the ball, practicing at home with practice swings and then hitting balls at the driving range and then playing with those cues.

Club Fitting: Jennifer's irons were too heavy and short. We replaced the irons with longer, lighter PING irons.

FocusBand: Jennifer practiced inside with putting and swinging and wore the FocusBand on the course. From the FocusBand feedback she learned how to recognize her right brain state and is learning to reproduce that state of mind on the course even without the FocusBand.

Outcome: Within the first week she was able to play on the golf course, staying clear and focused over the majority of shots. She began to identify when she was in her left or right brain. Her shot execution, putting, scoring, and joy improved as she continued to use the Focus Band.

Electrical Medical: Used Laser Touch One™ for elbow tendonitis.

Francesca   Collegiate Golfer • 4 Handicap • 20 years old

Learning Preference: Auditory/Visual primary and Tactile secondary. Left Brain preference.

Sensory Cues: Getting a tune in her head for the round. Tune varies. Sees shape of shot when preparing for shot. When over ball, focuses on back of ball. Stays over the shot a short time and executes the shot.

Physical Swing Work: Learning "lofted" and "cut" chipping shots. Confirming mechanics of all chipping shots to increase confidence and eliminate doubt and second thoughts over the shot. Confirming aspects of full swing to add to confidence and eliminate doubt. Balance in start and finish.

Club Fitting: Irons were irregular in lie angle and all needed lie angle adjustment to make them consistent. The shafts in her hybrids and fairway wood were too stiff and need to be replaced with shafts to match irons and driver shaft strength.

FocusBand: Francesca used the FocusBand for a week, on and off the course. She worked with the FocusBand with chipping and putting to gain more confidence and consistency.

Outcome: Confidence and scoring on the course improved substantially after a week of use with the FocusBand. She is continuing to use the FocusBand once or twice a day to practice recognizing her states of mind and being able to shift to right or left at will.

Tim   Professional Baseball Player • 7 Handicap • 26 years old

Learning Preference: Auditory primary and Tactile secondary. Left/Right Brain equal.

Sensory Cues: Sense of timing of transition from backswing to through swing. Maintaining sense of relaxation in hands from setup through the swing.

Physical Swing Work: Consistent start and finish in balance. Because his clubs were too short, he was often off balance at address and finish. With lengthened clubs, the address and finish position were more balanced and his ability to turn consistently with power increased.

Club fitting: Tim's irons, hybrids and fairway woods and Driver were too short. New longer, lighter irons were ordered at 2 inches over standard. Hybrids and Fairway woods were extended 2 inches. Driver was extended 1 inch.

FocusBand: Had a great experience with the FocusBand for his golf focus and also immediately saw the benefit to his baseball play.

Outcome: Accuracy of wedges and putting immediately improved. He had been over thinking and analyzing on those parts of his game. With longer clubs and a more balanced, powerful swing, he added length and accuracy to all his clubs.

Electrical Medical: Used Light Relief® and Laser Touch One™ for knee pain relief.

Paul   Business Development Executive • 8 Handicap • 70 years old

Learning Preference: Visual Left Brain Dominant.

Sensory Cues: Visualizes the ball flight prior to shot, usually as a dark grey line. Or could visualize target area where ball would land.

Physical Swing Work: Takeaway as part of core turning to take club back first 12 inches, quieting the hands in the takeaway. Learned to complete backswing. Had played with shorter, baseball like backswing, causing lack of core rotation on backswing and tendency to reverse pivot, having too much weight on forward foot at top of backswing position.

Club Fitting: Irons needed 1 inch extension. Added a 23-degree hybrid. Putter needed reshafting and loft adjustment for alignment issue.

FocusBand: After introduction he began to practice and play with the FocusBand. Paul practiced every day for 20 minutes with the FocusBand inside. When he played after a few weeks training he was able to keep his focus and eliminate the distractions that had been present in his previous rounds. He learned to recognize when he was in the right brain state for shot execution.

Outcome: Hitting more consistent driver, hitting more fairways. Putting and scoring are more consistent and shot lowest round ever.

Electrical Medical: Used Laser Touch One™ to treat thumb sprain. After a month of using the FocusBand he played five days of golf on a golf trip, all rounds better than before.

Shelley   Real Estate Executive • 2 years of golf experience • 50 years old

Learning Preference: Kinesthetic primary with Visual Secondary. Right Brain preference

Sensory Cues: Target focus and upper body with no tension. No thinking over ball. Establishing a golf shot routine with minimal time in set up over the ball.

Physical Swing Work: New golfer. Followed the swing learning outline in the book and the workbook. Balanced setup to balanced follow up first. Then perfected backswing and learning physics of ball flight. Practiced motions away from the ball to myelinate the swing. Will be finished with golf swing within the next few months. Practicing keeping the lower and upper body in sync on longer pitch shots added to her short game improvement.

Club Fitting: With advice from Gary Blaisdell, master club fitter, she gradually replaced her beginner set, a few clubs at a time. Eventually she had a full set of perfectly fit clubs. She has high hips and needed her clubs a half-inch longer.

FocusBand: After introduction she practiced inside and gradually adapted that to putting and the full swing. Learned to recognize when she was in the right brain state for shot execution.

Outcome: She loves learning and playing the game. She moved from 9 holes to 18 holes and then joined a playing association at two golf clubs. She set goals for scoring improvement that she has been achieving with the goal to be competitive in her club competitions.

AFTERWORD

Everyone plays golf for his or her own reasons.

No matter what those reasons are, everyone is seeking a pleasurable experience through playing or practicing the game. I always seek from my students the reasons that bring them to the game. And I always keep in mind that they are looking for a pleasurable experience. Some call it fun. Some call it competition. Some call it exercise. Some call it mind over matter. Whatever they seek, I want to help them find it so it is enjoyable.

Using the concepts in this book, I have watched hundreds of golfers find the joy they were seeking. As they learned more about themselves and learned how to better manage their brain, their experience became more pleasurable and they could repeat it.

I invite you to find your joy... by integrating the PMG System into your golf game.

.

Resources

BOOKS

How to Learn Anything Quickly: Quick, Easy Tips to Improve Memory, Reading Comprehension, Test-Taking Skills, and Learning through the Brain's Fastest Superlinks Learning Style
by Ricki Linksman (National Reading Diagnostics Institute, 1996 - 2001)

Every Shot Must Have a Purpose
by Lynn Marriott and Pia Nilsson (Gotham, 2005)

The Game Before the Game
by Lynn Marriott and Pia Nilsson (Gotham, 2007)

Play Your Best Golf Now
by Lynn Marriott and Pia Nilsson with Ron Sirak (Gotham, 2011)

The Natural Swing
by George Knudson (McClellan & Stewart, 1988)

The Body Electric
by Robert O. Becker, M.D. and Gary Selden (Harper, 1985)

The Talent Code
by Daniel Cole (Bantam Dell, 2009)

ARTICLES & VIDEOS

MYELINATION
"White Matter" by R. Douglas Fields | March 1, 2008 issue of *Scientific American*

FOCUSBAND / JASON DAY
https://www.youtube.com/watch?v=UQJedTChDz0

http://www.couriermail.com.au/sport/golf/masters-2015-brain-training-device-helping-aussie-jason-day-relax-and-focus/news-story/9f096ccca34 20271b10ea11e4461edbd

Praise for Kerry Graham, *The Power of Mental Golf* and Power Mental Golf

I have taken lessons from many good teachers. The system that Kerry has created is incredible—like no other instruction I have ever taken or heard of. My handicap went down 10 strokes in just three months. – Brandon T.

I'm over-the-top excited about your book!! Because of you I am confident and able to actually show up at any local course and play. I LOVE approaching the ball with only one thought. Adjusting all my golf clubs to fit me and all that you've shared with me during our handful of lessons has made "the difference" in my ability. – Kelly M.

After years of over-thinking and falling apart in the Big Pressure Situations, I have learned to stop the over-thinking and now play so much better under pressure. – Scott S.

I finally found how I can play naturally. I play a lot of sports and golf always seemed awkward and uncomfortable. I am tall and always wanted longer clubs. Now I have my longer clubs and can stand tall and the swing is so much easier. With clubs that fit and better mental organization, golf is now fun and so much more natural. – Danny W.

Approaching the ball with an organized thought process has helped me stay relaxed and find my natural swing. Thank you, Kerry! – Pam M.

I have worked with Kerry for over 10 years and her system has helped me take my junior golf career go to a higher level. Thanks to her I reached my goal of becoming a Division 1 student athlete! What's incredible about PMG is that it can be applied in other aspects of your life. I will forever be grateful for Kerry and her PMG system for changing my life! – Daffodil S.

Kerry has provided me with a more personal and engaging ownership of my golf game. Through a process of understanding my learning style, very simple, non-technical instruction, and single-thought focus during practice, I am playing my best golf with fun and confidence. – Brett E.

After many years of confusing lessons and frustrating rounds I was very close to giving up my golf game when a friend recommended Kerry to me. Hearing of my recent struggles and scores of 120 or more, my friend suggested I give Kerry a try—but I really wasn't interested in another lesson that would change yet another thing about my swing. It took me a few more aggravating rounds before I finally gave Kerry a call and today I am so grateful I found her! In just a few short months Kerry has helped me manage my thoughts, get my old natural golf swing back, and really enjoy the game again! I'm consistently shooting mid-to-low 90s now and truly believe scoring in the 80s is just around the corner! I have my game back, I'm having fun playing, and I am so very thankful for Kerry who helped me find my confidence and my love for the game again. – Cynde W.

Kerry allowed me to "own" my swing, keep it simple, stay in balance, visualize, and stay in the moment. When you learn to have fun with the "Kerry Method" and then get fitted to clubs that match your swing you will have a game you can enjoy for the rest of your life. Don't miss out! – Marv F.

I enjoy competitive golf. With Kerry's help I have improved my focus and my "self talk" is more positive. I have developed more confidence in my swing and lowered my handicap. I have really enjoyed our time together and I thank you for all your help. – Janet T.

I had given up golf for many years because of what I thought was a congenital slice when I happened to meet Kerry Graham. In 15 minutes she cured the slice and now has me firmly believing that the only problem with my golf game is between my ears and we are solving that together. – E.B.

I was a 4-handicap golfer and had a traumatic brain injury a few years ago. Kerry and her focus on mental strength has brought happiness back to my golf game. – Mike M.

As a college golfer embarking on a professional career, Kerry has given me the best gifts a teacher can give: security and independence. Kerry has given me peace of mind on the course that I have been given the right tools to teach myself and create a more powerful and effective mental game that has allowed me to understand my decision- making process better. She has given me the tools to coach myself in competition and get back on track when I fall off— which gives me the key to taking my game to the next level. – Jacquie L.

ABOUT THE AUTHORS
KERRY R. GRAHAM

Kerry Graham is a Life member of the Ladies Professional Golf Association (LPGA) Teaching and Club Professional (T&CP) membership. Her life has been dedicated to golf instruction and golf industry leadership.

Beginning in the 1970s, Kerry journeyed through the golf industry as an instructor, club fitter, college coach, golf shop merchandiser, country club manager, and golf course design team member. In 1985 Kerry entered into leadership of the LPGA, first as an LPGA T&CP Section President and Education Committee member and then, from 1987 to 1993, as National President of the Teaching & Club Professional Membership. During those six years, Kerry led initiatives to found the LPGA Girls Golf Club and the LPGA Urban Youth Golf Program (the forerunner of The First Tee), and led the LPGA Teaching Division to continue emphasis and improvement in the Teacher Training and Certification program.

In 1991, as National President, Kerry envisioned and initiated the first Women in Golf Summit, hosted by the LPGA in Orlando, Fla. Additional summits were held in 1993 and 1995. The objective of the summits was to define the issues and initiatives most important to women's golf in the 1990s. It gathered, for each of the three conferences, more than 400 men and women representing all aspects of the golf industry, including associations, golf management, manufacturing, travel and real estate, golf course design, media, college and high schools, professionals and amateurs. In 1995 Kerry received the National Golf Foundation's Joe Graffis Award for her dedication to growing the game through these summits.

Kerry has been a pioneer in leading changes in the golf industry. Her personal passion has always been to provide the best golf instruction to her clients. Through seminars and public speaking she has encouraged her golf professional colleagues, the golf professional organizations and the golf industry to become an advocate for better golf instruction training, certification and support.

Through the years Kerry has been recognized with many golf industry awards, including the Graffis Award for Education, the Patty Berg Award, the LPGA Commissioner's Award, the Women's Sports Foundation President's Award, and the LPGA Ellen Griffin Award. In 2005, Graham was inducted into the Arizona Golf Hall of Fame, and, in 2008, the LPGA T&CP Hall of Fame.

Beginning golf at nine years of age, Kerry Graham played junior golf competitively in the summers in Wyoming and then intercollegiate golf at Arizona State University. She earned a B.A. and a Master's Degree in Learning Psychology from Arizona State University and continued a journey to better understand and teach using the power of the mind.

Throughout, Kerry was especially interested in the mental aspects of the game of golf, integrating mental aspects into teaching and playing the game. She currently teaches golf in Phoenix, does public speaking and conducts seminars on The Power of Mental Golf. She continues to study all aspects of the game, both physical and mental, to improve her skills and service to her clients and has developed strategies to identify individuals' learning styles, keep instruction focused and simple, apply new technology, and assist each student to identify how to best accomplish their goals in learning and playing golf.

www.powermentalgolf.com

About the Authors
Ricki Linksman

Ricki Linksman is an author and leading expert in brain-based accelerated learning techniques for all types of learning and brain styles. She is the developer of one of the fastest brain-based memory and reading comprehension improvement, accelerated learning, learn to read, improve reading comprehension, and learn anything quickly program in the world today. Superlinks™ is a system she developed using neuroscience and brain research.

Ricki is also the founder-director of National Reading Diagnostics Institute, headquartered in Naperville, Illinois, near Chicago, a training institution to help people of all ages accelerate learning and improve their memory and reading comprehension through Superlinks™. The Institute trains instructors, sports, athletic, and life coaches, trainers, administrators, employers, professors, and teachers in any field to be more effective in their training roles.

She directs a parent center in which she offers reading diagnostic testing, learning and brain style inventory assessments to find one's fastest way of learning, serving students from pre-K, kindergarten, Grades 1 through Grades 12, college, and adult learners.

Her Keys to Reading Success™ program includes parent involvement worksheets to help parents be more effective in providing homework help. The Off the Wall Phonics™ games trains students (from beginning readers to those who want to improve word-reading to boost comprehension in elementary, middle, and high schools and colleges) to learn to master every phonics patterns in the English language in only 10 weeks through games.

She is the author of many books, including:

How to Learn Anything Quickly: Quick, Easy Tips to Improve Memory, Reading Comprehension, Test-Taking Skills, and Learning through the Brain's Fastest Superlinks Learning Style

The Fine Line between ADHD and Kinesthetic Learners: 197 Kinesthetic Activities to Quickly Improve Reading, Memory, and Learning in Just 10 Weeks: The Ultimate Parent Handbook for ADHD, ADD, and Kinesthetic Learners

How to Improve Memory Quickly by Knowing Your Personal Memory Style: Quick, Easy Tips to Improve Memory through the Brain's Fastest Superlinks Memory and Learning Style

Solving Your Child's Reading Problems

How to Improve Reading Comprehension Quickly by Knowing Your Personal Reading Comprehension Style: Quick, Easy Tips to Improve Comprehension through the Brain's Fastest Superlinks Learning Style

From ADHD or ADD to A's: Improve Reading, Memory, and Learning Quickly for Kinesthetic Learners

Ricki has been serving students in public and private schools throughout the country and around the world. Whenever she has set up the system of accelerated learning and accelerated reading in schools, those schools have raised test scores and achievement through her methods within less than one school year. Test scores raised include CTBS, SAT, ACT, and ISAT (Illinois State Achievement Test). Her program has also been used to prepare students for career examinations in diverse fields, such as medicine and law.

Ricki has worked as a consultant to golf instructors to improve teaching of golf through Superlinks to Accelerated Learning™ learning styles. She has trained football coaches to help football players improve learning the football playbook through Superlinks™ to help win games. Athletes use Superlinks™ to improve their learning of skills in many sports, including: basketball, baseball, and soccer. She has worked as a consultant to businesses, companies, and educational institutions to help people accelerate and improve learning in any field and she has done trainings for college professors and instructors at colleges and universities.

Ricki received the Certificate of Merit for IASCD's (Illinois Association for Supervision and Curriculum Development) WINN Research Certificate of Award of Merit for Outstanding Research.

For information on Ricki Linksman's books and services visit her websites:

http://www.readinginstruction.com

http://www.keystoreadingsuccess.com

http://www.keyslearning.com

http://www.superlinkslearning.com

http://www.nationalreadingdiagnosticsinstitute.com

http://www.offthewallphonics.com

NOTES

NOTES